Kerry Tyack's
Guide to
Breweries and
BEER
in New Zealand

NEW
HOLLAND

Published in 1999 by New Holland Publishers (NZ) Ltd
Auckland • Sydney • London • Cape Town

218 Lake Road, Northcote, Auckland, New Zealand
14 Aquatic Drive, Frenchs Forest, NSW 2086, Australia
24 Nutford Place, London W1H 6DQ, United Kingdom
80 McKenzie Street, Cape Town 8001, South Africa

ISBN 1 877246 09 3

Book production and design: Alison Dench
Managing editor: Renée Lang

Printed by Times Offset (M) Sdn Bhd, Malaysia

10 9 8 7 6 5 4 3 2 1

Contents

Acknowledgements   6
Preface   7
Introduction   9
Matching beer with food   11
How to use this book   16

North Island breweries
   Location map   17
   Breweries and their beers   18
South Island breweries
   Location map   81
   Breweries and their beers   82
Other New Zealand breweries   128
New Zealand beer labels   129

Imported beers   145

Glossary   167
References   170
Index   171

Acknowledgements

Thanks for their support and assistance are due to Hamish Riach and the Beer, Wine & Spirits Council, Sonia Rossiter at Rydges Hotel Group, David Cryer, Geoff Griggs, Matt Kane and especially Luke Nicholas. Thanks also to the brewers, big and small, around the country who gave freely of their time, their product and their experience to help me bring everything together.

Preface

Brewing, beer and the social history of New Zealand are inextricably linked. The story of beer in this country has not always been a happy one: from the early days the centuries-old craft of brewing has attracted the ire of sections of the community wanting to apply to beer the mantle of social pariah. New Zealand was never immune from the prohibitionists and even now there are still 'dry areas' in some cities. Beer, its production and its consumption are responsible for some of the most provocative legislation on the nation's law books.

At the same time as it has had its detractors, beer has played a significant role in shaping New Zealand society. Through the decades whole communities have been formed around a single brewery. Many families have attained fame and not inconsiderable fortune from brewing or selling beer. It remains a key element in much of our conviviality and our entertainment: it is almost always present at social gatherings involving celebration and commemoration. The bigger breweries, as well as touting their products, have continued to support community activities, sponsoring sport and cultural endeavour, and have been both courted and criticised for their efforts.

As we enter the new millennium things are changing, although the Kiwi love of beer is no less formidable. The guilt increasingly attached by some to its sensible and sensitive enjoyment is puzzling when you consider that drink-drive laws, the wider availability of beer and a more responsible attitude towards its serving and consumption have meant that New Zealand beer drinkers are considering what, where and how they drink much more carefully.

Something else has happened. Craft brewing has become far more visible and the range of products far more accessible. One commentator described it this way: '"Micro" breweries are now at the heart of an exciting and vibrant market that gives the consumer a wider selection than ever before.' He's right. Most of the beers reviewed in this guide come from small craft breweries. That is not to say they are the biggest sellers — far from it. Although the bigger breweries can still lay claim to the palates of the vast majority of beer drinkers, there is no doubt craft brews are gaining in popularity. Awareness of this fact is spurring more would-be brewers into action and encouraging even the larger brewers to look at the nature of product they are providing.

Not all of the smaller breweries are making high-brow, purist styles designed to confront the palate and steer drinkers towards diversity. Many are simply adding their version of mainstream beers to the list of what is available in their region. Others are unashamedly taking on the big breweries on quality and price. These midsize brewing companies, with shareholdings often made up of retailers and hoteliers, are making their own product more cheaply than they can source it from anyone else. In amongst all these is a group of talented, enthusiastic and sometimes critical brewers determined to produce beers in the European or British style. Their aim is to offer consumers a taste of 'real' beer and to educate them about what exists beyond lager, draught and dark.

Among the beers available in New Zealand we have brands that will last only until someone actually tastes them, and we have beers that have repeatedly won the highest international accolades. We have quaffers, we have speciality beers, we have high-strength and low-strength, hand-made and mass-produced. This guide celebrates this diversity and wishes it long life!

Introduction

I was attending a reunion of ex-colleagues not so long ago and mentioned to one that I was writing a guide to New Zealand beer. In an instant his eyes lit up and he began a chronicle of tales about his past life as a senior postmaster and how one of his jobs was to visit breweries to check the brewing gravity so that excise tax could be calculated. In one town, because there had been some trouble, this same postmaster had the only brewery key and no work could begin until he had opened up each morning. Such were the responsibilities of our most trusted citizens!

There aren't many people in New Zealand who, even if not directly affected at some stage in their lifetime, cannot at least tell a tale that relates to the brewing industry. I am no exception. As a young lad I looked forward to visiting with my grandparents in Te Awamutu. I still fondly recall travelling miles in Granddad's old flatbed Bedford to the far reaches of the Waikato and northern King Country to collect returnable brown bottles. Granddad had a contract with the ABC bottling company in Auckland to collect spent beer bottles, pack them, load them onto a railway wagon and send them back to be refilled.

Author Gordon McLauchlan delved further than anyone into the history of beer and brewing in New Zealand in his book *The Story of Beer*. There has been a host of books written on individual breweries, including Donald Gordon's history of Dunedin's historic Speight's. Others have conducted exhaustive searches and written highly detailed accounts of the brewing activity in a region. Frank Leckie's *Otago's Breweries: Past and Present* is a good example.

This guide is not of the same ilk. It is intended to be just what the title suggests — a guide to the breweries, the brewers and the beer you can find in this wonderful country. It is no great historical record, nor is it full of lush colour photography. It does not rate the beers it profiles. It simply provides current, comprehensive and concise details about where the breweries are, what beer they make and whether they are open to visitors. The guide also includes a list of the imported beers available here, should they be your preference.

Please don't leave this guide lying on the shelf somewhere out of sight. Shove it into the glovebox of your car or in your backpack so that, wherever you are, a quick check will tell you exactly what beer is available in the area.

The guide has another intended use. The focus on beer around the world is growing at an enormous rate. Frequently tourists who have an interest in beer are unable to find out even basic information about the beers brewed here. Some are not even aware we brew beer in New Zealand! This simple guide aims to fix all that. If you know of anyone visiting the country who takes an interest in local beers, make sure they know about the guide. Better still, buy them a copy and make a friend for life.

Finally I have included as many beer labels from New Zealand beers as I can. There are some stunning examples, creative, colourful and curious. For the collector these will be an eye-opener. For others they will add another dimension to a fascinating craft so admirably executed by some extremely talented brewers throughout the country.

Matching beer with food

'Beer has a special affinity to hearty, powerfully flavoured foods. The sweet earthiness of malt, bitter undertones of hops and bready flavours of the yeast combine to provide a rich matrix that absorbs and plays against spices, herbs, hot peppers and intense tastes. Where a delicate wine would be overwhelmed by a spicy dish, beer digs in and fights back.'

Bruce Aidells and Denis Kelly, Real Beer and Good Eats

The concept is simple: if you choose the right beer to accompany the right food, your enjoyment of both will be enhanced. But convincing the average Kiwi that it is *de rigueur* to mix haute cuisine with the much-loved brown stuff is a big, if not enormous, ask. However let's not let that daunt us — pairing beer with food is still something well worth considering.

The pairing of beer and food is neither new nor peculiar. Brewhouses, cafés and wayside inns have been around for centuries and they have always, always involved food. Wherever beer is served in Europe we see counter lunches, pies, ploughman's lunches, biersticks, beer batter, beer bread, pizza and so on. You have only to look at the art of Bruegel and other European masters to see how often the tankard of ale was set down beside the roast game or the platter of bread and cheese. Basic, hearty fare was the order of the day and while today the food options are much broader the exploration of the combinations remains as valid.

Beer drinkers' palates are changing and developing, becoming more sensitive as tasters become more knowledgeable. Drinkers are taking time to sample and savour different brands, to appreciate the style and aroma, to distinguish between flavours and to appreciate the craftsmanship that provides strong, individual characteristics in each beer. A logical step in this process is the restoration of beer to its rightful place in our lives, making it once again a valid option when looking for a beverage to accompany and enhance meals.

When matching beer with food there are some important things to keep in mind. It can be as complex, as tantalising, varied and exciting as matching wine with food. As with wine matching, no one beer will combine with all food in a way that satisfies everyone's palate. Most beers go with most food, but finding a superb beer/food match is more of a challenge. The quest is for synergy — neither the beer nor the food should overwhelm the other. They should be better in combination than they are apart. Pairing beer and food is subjective, so no opinion is right — however there are some clear rules that will assist those thinking of giving it a go.

It is likely that beer styles from different regions will combine best with the cuisine styles of the same region. There is good reason for this. Boutique brewers have been the rule as opposed to the exception around the world, so beer — until the advent of modern transportation — has always had a strong regional connection. Beer was made in small batches by home and village brewers, and these craftsmen used local ingredients and were subject to local brewing conditions. Consequently the flavour of these beers reflected the local *terroir*, to borrow a hip winemaking term.

In this the development of beer has mirrored that of cuisine. But while there has been an enormous increase in the acceptance of international brands, many beers still have their greatest support close to home. It is logical therefore to look first at local cuisine to find what scope there is for finding that ideal combination.

Now, as with wine, there is a huge element of personal preference in all this. There are no right or wrong answers. However, to get the best out of the experience it is worthwhile taking time to consider what makes a better-than-average combination.

The tasting

All styles of beer have completely individual textures, aromas and flavours. They all affect the palate differently and our senses react to each of them differently. Every beer is made using a different recipe and between them they cover every element and facet of the flavour spectrum.

So get to know something about beer. Learn to distinguish a lager from a pilsener, Guinness from stout. Find out more about brewing and the processes that contribute to the taste profiles. Build up a vocabulary of appropriate terms so that, when discussing beer, you are able to share your thoughts about the flavours you pick up.

Get in the habit of presenting a beer at its best. The temperature should be around 8°C, although typically in New Zealand beer is drunk at around 3–4°C. Serve a good-quality beer in a good-quality glass. While appearance is not important when matching a beer with food, it is part of the enjoyment to see the appropriate colour, clarity and head for the beer style. The glass should be clear and cleaned of any soap residue.

Aroma is very important because our sense of smell is so closely tied into our sense of taste. Take time to lift the glass to your nose and form an opinion as to what smells you can identify. Common characteristics are the flowery and herbal nose of a well-brewed lager and the maltiness of a Bavarian-style beer. Often ales leave an impression of fruitiness.

Flavour, naturally, is the most important characteristic. Taking into account the influence of each ingredient and the particular beer style on the final product will definitely aid in the food-matching process. Begin with a generous mouthful and swirl it around so that it covers all the palate before swallowing.

The 'body' of a beer, as with wine, ranges from thin to full with the same general matching principles. The perceived thickness of a beer comes from its grain to water ratio. Carbonation should also be considered because an overly effervescent beer hampers the ability of the palate to taste. Look for a smooth, elegant, complex finish and note whether it quickly disappears or lingers a little.

The matching

When pairing beer and food the choices are as complex as you want them to be, but the end result can be simply wonderful. Many beers make excellent aperitifs as the bitterness produced by the hops stimulates the appetite by increasing the production of gastric juices. The chemistry of the mouth is changed a great deal by food and one's appreciation of the beer changes accordingly. The main thing is to keep it simple — match like with like.

When considering a menu for your guests think about dishes that emphasise wholesome, natural ingredients in keeping with the entirely natural ingredients and processing involved in the making of beer. Try to achieve a high degree of compatibility between the beer and the menu in terms of texture, flavour and balance.

The less sweet the food, the drier the beer should be. Pair a delicate shellfish dish with a pale ale or mild lager, which are made using light and subtle ingredients. If you increase the seasoning or choose more strongly flavoured ingredients, the beer should also be more intense, perhaps an amber ale or dark lager. Darker beers — porters and stouts — all beautifully balance red meats in rich sauces and gravies. They also go well with savoury spiced meats like corned beef or a traditional pot roast.

Beer is a perfect foil for ethnic, especially spicy, cuisines. Water only spreads the chilli around, but it is tremendously refreshing to wash down hot food with a pilsener, a light amber or mild wheat beer. The higher the alcohol content, the more soothing the beer will be.

How to use this book

The list of New Zealand breweries is set out geographically from North to South and includes all breweries currently registered here. My intention was to visit each brewery, talk to the brewers and assemble the required information. Unfortunately constraints of finding mutually acceptable dates and times, flash floods (northernmost breweries), distance (the Chatham Islands) and the reluctance of some brewers to talk to me meant I was not entirely successful. However I did visit the vast majority of the working breweries. I have also listed the names and addresses of one or two breweries that, whilst operating (or close to it) at the time of writing, had no beer available for me to try. Consider these an unknown quantity and seek them out to create your own impressions.

The tasting notes for each brewery are given in the order I tasted the beer. Treat them as a guide only. I formed my impressions during a single tasting of a single batch, and brewing is an ever-evolving craft, an art form. For many of the craft brewers I spoke to, change is part of the pain and part of the pleasure of brewing. On the day you may form a different view to mine. That's okay. In fact it is more than that: it's exactly how it should be.

 Look out for beers marked with this rosette: they were gold medal winners at the inaugural New Zealand Hop Marketing Board International Beer Awards in 1999.

Lastly, when you visit those breweries that are open to the public, seek out the brewer and offer him or her encouragement. Ask those questions, provide that feedback. It's what many of them thrive on and need to keep them positive about the value of their effort.

North Island breweries

Hokianga Breweries

Northland Breweries

Burkes
Pilot Bay

Waiheke Island Microbrewery

Rangitoto
Brofords
Bean Rock
Loaded Hog
Shakespeare
Malthouse
Lion Breweries
Galbraith

Australis
Trident
Onehunga Spring
Waitemata Brewery
Auckland Breweries
Steam Brewing Co.
Independent Brewery

Kahikatea

Sunshine

White Cliffs

Brew Haus

O'Neills

Coastal

Independent Brewery
The Brewhouse

Roosters

Shamrock

Tui

Parrot & Jigger
Polar

Burridges

Loaded Hog

Hokianga Breweries

ADDRESS SH 12, Waimamaku, Kaikohe **PHONE** (09) 405 8681
FAX (09) 405 8681 **BREWER** Innes Carrad **OPEN** 10 am–6 pm daily

Hokianga Breweries, in the far north of the North Island, is the pride and pleasure of Innes Carrad and his family. Innes, a keen home-brewer, decided his beer was good enough to be shared with the locals and tourists who called in to the small family café on the Hokianga Harbour. He bought the historic butcher's shop next door and created Hokianga Breweries. The staple beer is Coachman's Ale, but Innes brews an occasional lager and dark beer to complement the range. Light meals are available to enjoy with your beer in the café or you can take some beer home in 745-millilitre bottles or 2-litre pets.

Coachman's Ale 4% abv

This dark brown beer has an easily distinguishable hop aroma that is derived from the Halletau hops used in its production. You will also find some malt fruit character in the bouquet. The texture is crisp and clean and the flavour is very malt driven, with plenty of fruitiness to balance a double dose of hops. It has good mouth-feel and plenty of length. Choose a mixed grill from the menu for a good match.

Northland Breweries

ADDRESS 104 Lower Dent Street, Town Basin, Whangarei **PHONE &**
FAX (09) 438 4664 **BREWER** Rick Mason **OPEN** 9 am–6 pm Mon–Sat

Northland Breweries is located in the heart of the Town Basin complex in Whangarei — a popular tourist stop for those visiting Northland and the Bay of Islands. The brewery produces three beers, all of them in the mainstream style: a lightly hopped pale lager, an American-style amber ale and a dark brown 'old ale'. The beer is available at many clubs and bars throughout Northland as well as from Northland Breweries itself.

Burkes Kaipara Brewery

ADDRESS 88 Commercial Road, Helensville **PHONE** (09) 420 7984 **FAX** (09) 420 8869 **BREWER** John Burke **OPEN** 11 am–7 pm Mon– Thurs, 11 am–8 pm Fri & Sat

Burkes Kaipara Brewery was established in 1994 by John Burke, a local dairy farmer looking for a change in lifestyle. John produces three beers on the premises, all designed to appeal to the locals who shop at his wholesale liquor store in the heart of this small regional centre 40 kilometres north of Auckland. They are typical of the beer styles preferred by the average Kiwi drinker — easy-drinking, lightweight with subtle flavours and tending towards sweetness. An unusual aspect of John's brewing process is the extended maturation time given to the beer.

Kaipara Gold Lager 4% abv

This is a pale straw, lager-style beer, lightweight with no significant aroma or flavour profile. It is sweet with a hint of the malt used coming through as well as a slight smokiness — although no toasted malt is used. It is a typical quaffing brew to enjoy in very hot weather when thirst quenching is the order of the day. Try it with spicy food like chicken satay.

Kaipara Olde Ale 4% abv

Dark red in colour with lots of caramel aromas and distinctive maltiness coming through, this ale is light and clean with a good head. On the palate it is smoky with a lingering bitterness similar to that of burnt coffee. This is the most popular brew with John's regular customers — they obviously enjoy the dark fruitcake character. It is best drunk with a hearty roast or used to enrich a gravy.

Burkes Bitter 4% abv

This attractive-looking beer is dark golden brown in colour, reminding me of golden syrup. The aroma is very light with no predominant character coming through. It is a lightweight version of bitter beer, with a sweet start and a very bitter/dry finish — almost sour — that will appeal to those who like a drier style. It pairs best with dishes that have a sweet element to offset the bitterness.

Pilot Bay Brewing Company

ADDRESS 1171 Coatesville–Riverhead Highway (SH 28), Riverhead, Auckland **PHONE** (09) 412 8595 **FAX** (07) 412 7755 **E-MAIL** service@riverheadest.co.nz **BREWER** Jim Dowling **OPEN** 9 am–6 pm Mon–Sat

The team at Pilot Bay, located at Riverhead Estate winery northwest of Auckland, brews the traditional way: slowly, carefully and using only malted barley, hops, yeast and water. No chemicals, preservatives or sugars are added and Pilot Bay beers are allowed to mature for at least a month. The beer is lightly carbonated, so you won't feel uncomfortable after a few. Jim Dowling says his aim is to produce beers that will be enjoyed by the majority of drinkers, as well as challenging their perceptions and understanding of beer. Jim plans to introduce a range of lambic and fruit beers; in the meantime Pilot Bay is available directly from the brewery and from selected liquor merchants, restaurants, bars and clubs throughout the country.

Pilot Bay Lager 4% abv

Mid-straw in colour (although light gold may be a better description), this beer has a very mild aroma and a smooth, crisp texture in the style of European lager. Renowned beer writer Michael Jackson liked its light flavour and slightly malt caramel aftertaste, although I feel that while there is a welcome hint of hop bitterness on the back palate a bit more length would cement its character. A good quaffing lager sure to be a popular choice on a hot day, it is a good match with spicy food — perhaps Cajun fish from the barbecue.

Pilot Bay Amber 4% abv

It's a golden brown colour, with lots of malt sweetness and soft hints of golden syrup in the aroma. The mouth-feel is good, the texture creamy without being cloying. The malt comes through again in the flavour and there is very mild hop influence. A well-balanced brown beer with good level of flavour, it is another favourite with the 'Kiwi beer' drinker and a sure hit as a session beer. Enjoy it with a mixed grill.

Pilot Bay Dark 4% abv

This has a deep amber colour just short of black. The aroma is sweet with some caramel/chocolate influences as well as some coffee. The texture is thin and crisp with light mouth-feel. The flavour is of chocolate and Christmas fruit and malt sweetness comes through as well. Well balanced and eminently drinkable, it's an appropriate introduction to this style of dark beer. Try it with a roast or — for something slightly more daring — serve it with a generous slice of dark chocolate cake.

Scottish Wee Heavy 5% abv

Brewed with Scottish malted barley, this beer is a medium brown colour with a slight red tinge. The aroma is of caramel and cold coffee with some fruitiness evident as well. The texture is smooth on the front with a slight graininess on the sides and back of the palate. It is full and flavourful with plenty of malt sweetness, some caramel and the merest hint of hop flavour towards the back of the palate. This is my pick of the Pilot Bay brews, more complex and challenging than the others. It's a good food beer, worth the effort of preparing something special — a hearty rabbit casserole with lots of root vegetables for me.

Original Manuka Honey Beer 4.8% abv

Surprise surprise, this one's honey coloured — medium straw with a touch of gold. A honey sweetness comes through in the aroma, the texture is creamy and the mouth-feel light. In flavour terms this beer is very mild with a light hand being used to add the manuka honey. This beer will appeal to the sweet tooth and be a welcome refresher served quite cold in the summer months. Try it with sweet and sour pork from your favourite Chinese food outlet.

Waiheke Island Microbrewery

ADDRESS 82 Onetangi Road, Waiheke Island, Auckland **PHONE** (09) 372 1014 **BREWER** Alan Knight

One of the newest craft breweries in the country, the 1200-litre Waiheke Island Microbrewery rolled out its first keg in January 1998. Since then its beers have gained wide distribution around the island, at Galbraith's Ale House in Auckland and at other outlets as far south as Wellington. In the future, product will be available from the brewery itself. Owners John and Megan Wallace and Bill and Debra Lyttle say their goal is to brew good-quality 'patio' beer that will satisfy the islanders and the many tourists who visit during the year and who are seeking food and beverage products unique to Waiheke. They have charged brewer Alan Knight with producing 'interesting ales with mass appeal'. The beers are sold under the Baroona label, Baroona being the name of a ferry that plied the Auckland–Waiheke route for many years. If visiting the island just ask for the Baroona Boys and everyone will immediately know who and what it is you want!

Baroona Original 4.7% abv

Baroona Original is yellow-gold in colour and has a mild malt and citrus aroma. The texture is smooth and clean with medium to full mouth-feel. The flavour evokes malt fruitiness with some citrus — grapefruit in particular. There is some hop very mildly evident, though it is more floral and lemony than bitter. There is reasonable finish with a pleasant dryness on the back palate. A very big seller, this is a nicely balanced beer with wide appeal. I would serve it with most spicy foods — perhaps a Thai chicken curry.

Baroona Berry 3.5% abv

Golden-tan in colour with a distinctive pink blush, this beer is one for summer drinking. It is a light wheat beer with strong berryfruit and melon aromas that come through equally clearly in the flavour. Add to this some mild wheat characteristics and you have a refreshing drink best served very cold. The texture is crisp and clean and there is some dryness on the back palate, which makes it an attractive aperitif. Alternatively you could serve it for a patio lunch with a fresh fruit salad.

Baroona Dark Ale 4% abv

This is a dark red-brown beer that, complete with creamy head, looks attractive in the glass. It has a really chocolatey bouquet and there is some malt fruit there as well to sweeten the aroma. It's not as creamy as some dark beers, rather it is crisp and clean with good mouth-feel. The flavour is predominantly chocolate as well, but there is enough hop there to provide a balancing dryness/bitterness on the back. It is in the porter style and the lighter texture works to carry the flavour. It is tempting to serve it with Waiheke Island oysters, but I would go further and make up a seafood platter that includes lashings of fresh crayfish!

Baroona Spring Pale Ale 5.5% abv

Copper-gold in colour with a slight cloudiness and big bubbles, this pale ale has an aroma that is full-on malt. The texture is creamy and fresh with good mouth-feel. On the palate there is a balanced mix of tropical fruit, hop flavour and some sweetness. It also has a mild hint of barley, which adds to both texture and flavour. There is plenty of length, with some dryness and some bitterness right at the end. It is a good example of the India pale ale style. When considering your food-match options think chicken first — or perhaps some creamy smoked fish.

Waiheke Winter Warmer 8% abv

A seasonal beer in a very attractive champagne-style bottle, Winter Warmer is very dark amber in colour — and a touch cloudy when shaken because of the yeast sediment in this unfiltered beer. It has a full, Christmas-fruit aroma with hints of strawberries and port. There is plenty of body to this beer, it is creamy and smooth and it fills the mouth generously. The flavour is fruity, quite sweet and spicy with hints of toffee, caramel and molasses, and the port character comes through again. A big beer for supping rather than a thirst quencher, it is perfect as a night-cap or served with a meal of roast beef with rich gravy.

Rangitoto Brewing Company

ADDRESS 134 Hurstmere Road, PO Box 33-043, Takapuna, Auckland
PHONE (09) 486 6330 **FAX** (09) 486 6333 **BREWER** Amanda Oades
OPEN 11 am–1 am Mon–Fri, 9 am–1 am Sat & Sun

Rangitoto Brewing Company is part of R'Toto Pub & Café, a popular eating and drinking venue on Auckland's busy North Shore. Located in the heart of Takapuna, the brewery services the needs of R'Toto as well as a number of other bars in the area. Brewer Amanda Oades says her goal is to give customers what they want to drink — plus some interesting 'options'. As a result her brews are best described as mainstream, although the quality is such that they are far from being ordinary. The interesting names given to the beers relate to the company logo and to the Rangitoto volcano itself. The beers are all available on tap at R'toto.

Lava Lager 4% abv
Light golden in colour with a mild hop and yeasty aroma, this lager has a crisp and clean texture with plenty of good, mouth-filling body. At first the flavour seems sweet and honey-like, but as you continue there are definite hay and freshly mown grass influences, and a

medium hop bitterness. It does not have a huge length but makes pleasant drinking all the same. This is R'Toto's biggest seller and matches well with sushi.

Crater Ale 4.5% abv

Tan-gold in colour, Crater is an easy-drinking ale with lots of malt sweetness in the aroma, which also comes through as the dominant flavour. The texture is smooth and slightly oily, and the flavour is malty with some fruit and nougat evident. This beer finishes early with a clean and fresh result. It easily fits into the mainstream Kiwi brown-beer style and will be best enjoyed with home-made cottage pie.

Black Rat Dark Ale 4.5% abv

This beer is, as you would expect, very dark brown in colour — with a slight amber hue. There is lots of chocolate and toffee character in the aroma, with a touch of tropical fruit. As it warms there is also a smoky influence. Mouth-feel is smooth and a little creamy with plenty of length. Slight coffee and Christmas-fruit flavours dominate, giving it a porter-like quality. A complex beer with a fascinating aroma and good length, enjoy it with a steak and kidney pie.

Raspberry Rat 4% abv

An interesting light lager, Raspberry Rat is light straw in colour with a slight blush when held to the light. Not surprisingly the dominant aroma is of raspberry, with some marshmallow and fruit jube characters as well. The texture is soft and creamy without being spritzy, the flavour mild raspberry with some woodiness as well. Basically what you smell is what you taste. A real favourite with women, this refreshing beer is ideal in summer with antipasto or fresh fruit salad.

Lava Lite 2.5% abv

With this beer, a real find, Amanda shows that it is possible to brew a low-alcohol beer with genuine flavour. Straw-gold in colour with a touch of lime, it has an aroma that is sweet with mild hop and some citrus character. The texture is crisp and clean with good mouth-feel. The taste is mild but true hop and malt flavours are evident and the hop bitterness on the finish is welcome. It is an excellent example of the style and, like most lagers, is appropriately served with dishes that have some spice — but as an alternative I would whip up a batch of sweetcorn fritters and serve them with Lava Lite and sambal.

Brofords Beers

ADDRESS 13 Bruce McLaren Road, Henderson **PHONE** (09) 837 2751
BREWERS Dave Hoyle & Steve Alexander **OPEN** 9 am–6 pm Mon–Fri, 10 am–6 pm Sat

Brofords Beers in West Auckland has for ten years serviced the needs of local customers through sales from the brewery and through the local licensing trusts. The beer reflects the palate preferences of Brofords' loyal customer base. It is naturally fermented and brewed with no added sugars, and is considered mainstream. The brewery is located in a light industrial centre in Henderson, and attached to it is a retail liquor store offering all Brofords' beers in 2-litre flagons, in stubbies and in kegs by arrangement.

 FACT The Sumerians drank their beer through straws that were hollow stalks of corn.

Brofords Western Lager 4% abv

Mid-straw in colour and on the day with a slight chill-haze, this beer has no aroma to speak of when cold but at room temperature wafts of cold tea appear. The texture is light and clean, the flavour mild with some citrus notes, some ginger and some hop bitterness showing through. A very mild lager style that will match well with steamed mussels with garlic and tomato.

Brofords Western Bitter 4% abv

This beer is rose-gold in colour and has a thick, creamy head when first poured. There are suggestions of tropical fruit and some honey in the aroma, which change into a prevailing smell of hot lemon drink. It has a creamy texture and mild malt flavours with a bit of fruit and some caramel. On the back palate there is a little hop bitterness to keep things interesting. Quite true to the style, it needs a sweeter dish to add balance — say chicken liver pâté.

Buchanan's Special Dark Ale 4% abv

Amber tending towards brown in colour, this beer has a distinct aroma of honey and dried mango. In the mouth it has a soft creaminess to it that lingers and carries the subtle flavours to the end. You will find hints of malt and some citrus coming through, but the hop influence is negligible. This is a light quaffer to drink with your pork chops.

Black Brute Stout 4% abv

In the glass this beer is deep, deep amber, and it gives off a strong aroma of cold coffee, caramel and some burnt-malt character. Another very finely textured beer with minimum mouth-feel, the stout hits the middle palate with tastes of Marmite and smoky malt. There is little length to take this flavour further and the beer probably won't satisfy the real stout-lovers. Try it with lamb shanks and kumara to add another dimension.

Charles Stolberg Premium Reserve Lager 4% abv

Another pale straw offering, this one has no aroma to speak of and a very light and clean texture that offers no great mouth-feel. The flavour too is very mild with only the merest hint of malt and hop. It is a very simple beer offering no great challenge to the palate and no real length. It will wash down a curry admirably.

Hooker Ale 7.5% abv

A strong, pale straw beer in the ale style, this one has some fruit, a bit of honey and lots of banana evident in the aroma. The texture is creamy and there is plenty of mouth-feel, although, in keeping with other Brofords beers, the flavour should be considered mild. There is some hop influence there and the tropical-fruit/banana character comes through too. Tempting as it is to serve this as an aperitif, I would also serve it with pasta with lots of sun-dried tomatoes, basil, capsicum and olives.

Bean Rock Brewing Company

ADDRESS 79 Ardmore Road, PO Box 46-266, Herne Bay, Auckland
PHONE (09) 376 3222 **FAX** (09) 376 3735 **BREWER** Brian Watson

Thousand of litres of beer went down the drain before Bean Rock Lager was pronounced fit for the market by Auckland-based entrepreneur Richard Holden. Produced at Independent Brewery under the steady hand of brewmaster Brian Watson, Bean Rock is in the genre of European-style lagers. Named after an icon of Auckland's Waitemata Harbour, Bean Rock is widely available in packaged form from retail outlets from Taupo north.

Bean Rock Lager 4.5% abv

Mid-straw in colour and with a hop and citrus aroma, this beer has broad appeal. The texture is clean and crisp and there is good mouth-feel and good length. On the palate it is moderately bitter with some fruit and cut-grass influences, as well as a touch of citrus towards the end. There is also enough residual sweetness to offer good balance, although the hop promise of the aroma does not last long enough to satisfy the real hop-head — the Original Bitter version of the same beer is more likely to please that lot. A good beer to enjoy with hot and spicy food — say Cajun chicken.

The Loaded Hog Brewery

ADDRESS Viaduct Quay, 104 Quay Street, Auckland City **PHONE** (09) 366 6491 **FAX** (09) 366 6495 **BREWERS** Mike McLean & Carl Day **OPEN** 11 am–late daily

The Loaded Hog is New Zealand's biggest restaurant/bar group, with seven outlets from Auckland to Dunedin. Each venue is strongly themed with a stylish decor focusing on rural New Zealand. The group prides itself on fast, efficient service in an environment that is lively and inviting. A full menu is available at each venue and an integral feature of each bar is the award-winning beers produced in three breweries strategically located to service all Loaded Hog outlets. The on-tap range is the same in each venue, and pigoon (the Loaded Hog's quirky name for riggers or pets) and keg sales are available. The Auckland brewery services the Loaded Hog in Hamilton.

Hog Gold Lager 4% abv

Yellow-gold, the colour of dry hay, this very popular lager has a mild aroma of grass, honey and hay. The body, in true American lager fashion, is crisp and clean, and there is no great finish. The flavour is mild, with some honey sweetness and a very slight hop bitterness. It's an easy-to-drink, mildly flavoured offering that is sure to have a large following. Uncomplicated and inoffensive, it is a well-made example of its style and a good food beer. I would serve it with a mild curry or a generous bowl of chilli con carne.

Hog Draft Beer 4% abv

An inviting, dark brown colour and a thick, creamy head provide the first impressions of this mainstream Kiwi draught. There is a mild malt sweetness to the aroma, with evidence of Christmas fruit. The mouth-feel is generous, while the texture is crisp and clean. Malt sweetness dominates the flavour but a distinct dryness on the back palate adds a dimension. This is a well-balanced beer with obvious appeal to the average Kiwi brown-beer drinker. It is pleasant drinking at the best of times, but for added pleasure serve it with a hearty roast-beef sandwich with pickles, mustard and all the trimmings!

Hog Dark Ale 4% abv

Very dark ruby in colour with a thick, creamy head, this beer has an aroma that is full of chocolate with additional mild molasses and coffee influences. It has a medium texture, creamy with a slightly grainy mouth-feel. It's fresh and mouth-filling, with dark fruit flavours and suggestions of molasses, and yeast and Marmite characters. This is a good example of a dark beer with the texture to carry the flavours through to the back palate. Serve it with black pudding or, for a contrast, fresh Orongo Bay oysters.

Hog Wheat Beer 4% abv

The brewer tells me this orange-gold beer is the favourite of Loaded Hog staff. It has no great aromatics but there is evidence of some tropical fruit and a hint of barley/wheat, as well as some biscuit influence (which may be why the young staff like it!). Very soft in texture and equally mild in flavour, it has no great length. It offers little challenge to the palate but is an easy drink at any time of the year. It's hard to pick a food that won't overpower it, but try whole fish (snapper or hoki) baked with some slices of lemon and seasoned with freshly ground pepper.

Shakespeare Tavern & Brewery

ADDRESS 61 Albert Street, Auckland City **PHONE** (09) 373 5396 **FAX** (09) 373 5397 **BREWER** Barry Newman **OPEN** 11.30 am–late daily **TASTINGS** by request

The Shakespeare brewery is located within the Shakespeare Tavern, one of central Auckland's older licensed premises. It is the site of New Zealand's first modern mini-brewery, and brewing takes place right in front of bar patrons. Affable brewer Barry Newman is considered a doyen of craft brewing in New Zealand. Barry is astute enough to understand what his patrons want in a beer and clever enough to brew beer that rises well above the average and introduces his regulars and the many tourists to a variety of beer styles. He uses a traditional batch-brewing process to ensure a continual supply of unfiltered and non-pasteurised beers for the enjoyment of patrons. Ask about Barry's seasonal and special beers when visiting the Shakespeare. The beer is also available to take away in 2-litre pets.

FACT The ancient Mesopotamians and Egyptians enjoyed beer. They drank a mixture of barley bread that was crumbled into water and fermented with date juice flavoured with cumin, myrtle, ginger and honey. The Gauls, Celts and Saxons produced beer that did not contain hops.

Barraclough Lager 4.1% abv

A bright straw-gold in colour, this lager is highly aromatic with lots of hop influence and some grassy notes — most likely from the dry-hopping used in its production. The texture is crisp and clean, while the flavour is sweetish to begin then filled with hop flavour and with plenty of residual hop bitterness on the finish. It's a well-balanced, fresh beer with full and generous use of hops. Top of my lager list, it's a very good food beer. Serve it up with braised pig trotters.

Shylock's Light 3.0% abv

This beer is a sparkling copper-gold colour with a malty aroma that has some molasses character. In the mouth it is crisp and clean with plenty of freshness. The malt comes through as flavour as well, but there is plenty of hop there too — and a little hint of ginger and spice to boot. Overall this is a very well-balanced, lower-strength beer with good mouth-feel and a tight, dry finish. Don't be faint-hearted with your food match: this beer will stand a solid, red-meat meal. Odds on it will go great with Mexican tacos or burritos.

Shakespeare Draught 4% abv

An appealing yellow-gold colour and a very mild aroma make this an interesting beer from the start. Best described as a mainstream draught, it has a smooth texture and creamy mouth-feel. There is plenty of malt character in the flavour but it is not overly sweet, with good hop influence as well. There is fruit but it doesn't dominate and the result is a pleasing and popular New Zealand brown-beer style that is great at a barbecue and equally at home with a winter hotpot.

Macbeth's Real Ale 4% abv
Ruby-red with a mild malt aroma and a rich, creamy texture, this beer does not have such timid malt in the flavour. It's big and full and casts its clear influence over the palate with a pleasant dryness on the back and a good, round finish. It's a rich, flavourful beer that has an appealing texture: not thin, not overly creamy. One for the more adventurous draught drinkers, it is another good Shakespeare food beer — a piece of gently grilled Scotch fillet or a venison steak will make an excellent match.

Falstaff's Real Ale 4.3% abv
In the glass this is a red-gold beer with a thick, creamy head. It is highly aromatic, with hops taking centre stage and some tropical fruit waiting in the wings. It is fresh and creamy in texture and the mouth-feel is generous. You immediately taste the sweetish fruit influence, some caramel and the hop bitterness as well. It is a complex beer, with well-balanced flavours and an excellent, satisfying finish. I really like this beer and look forward to serving it with duck roasted with stonefruit.

Willpower Stout 4% abv
This stout is a very dark, almost black beer with a thick, creamy head. A little surprisingly, it has a very mild aroma with just a hint of molasses and fruit mince. The texture is soft and creamy with a

freshness that's appealing in this style. The flavour is malty with some roasted and bitter-chocolate influences. Soft coffee and chocolate hints are also there, just to keep it interesting. It has good flavour balance, though it's the texture that sets this example of the style apart. As this stout is good with cheese, consider trying it with a blue-cheese soufflé.

King Lear Old Ale 7.5% abv

Full bodied, full strength and full on, this beer is not for the faint-hearted! It is deep, deep amber-brown with a thick, creamy head. The aroma is quite mild with malt sweetness coming through as well as some dried fruit and coffee. The texture is thick, rich and creamy. The flavour is full and sweet on the front — some toffee, some chocolate — with nicely balanced hop bitterness on the back. A thoroughly pleasant supping ale to enjoy before a meal, it is equally good as a fireside finish to an evening.

The Malthouse Brewery & Bar

ADDRESS 2/501 Karangahape Road, Auckland **PHONE** (09) 358 1311
FAX (09) 358 3307 **BREWER** Charles Kumar **OPEN** from 9 am daily

The Malthouse Brewery & Bar is located in a shopping and office complex on one of Auckland's busiest central-city streets. The premises are fully licensed and a range of drinks and a full menu are available. Brewer Charles Kumar says his goal is to brew beer that will appeal to a broad spectrum of customers, both men and women. He says that because the beer is only available at the Malthouse the preferences of regular customers are very important. Charles's beers fit comfortably into the mainstream category and they are designed to cater for traditionalists as well as those new to beer drinking.

Malthouse Lager 4% abv

Pale straw in colour, this beer has a sweet aroma with a hint of honey and lime. The texture is creamy and a little grainy. The sweetness of the aroma does not transfer to the flavour, which is very citric, almost sour. While the finish is fairly short, it does have a distinct dryness on the back of the palate that some will find attractive. It's certainly in the lager style and will match with spicy food, although I think it will be best served with something sweeter to balance the bitter notes.

Malthouse Real Ale 4% abv

The colour of this ale is tan-gold and the aroma demonstrates some fruitiness, but the overriding impression is of a hay shed — grassy and dry — which comes from the hops. It has good mouth-feel, being creamy and smooth, and the flavour is mildly fruity with some quickly passing hop bitterness on the back. A very sweet offering that will appeal to those who like a decent session beer, it is also ideal with grilled meat and salad.

Malthouse Dark 4% abv

As you'd expect, this beer is a dark chocolate-brown. It has an aroma of coffee and roasted malt, and the texture is light and thin with a certain freshness about it. This beer needs to be at room temperature for best effect: the flavour then reminds me of cold coffee and chocolate. It is quite bitter and there is not much sign of malt sweetness past the tip of the tongue. It is standard dark ale of a type that appears to be growing in popularity around the country, a bit light for blue cheese but good with red meat.

Lion Breweries (New Zealand Breweries)

ADDRESS 5–7 Kingdom Street, Newmarket, Auckland **PHONE**
(09) 377 8840 **FAX** (09) 358 8587 **WEBSITE** www.lion-nathan.co.nz
TOURS 10.30 am & 2 pm Tue–Thu; bookings essential

Three breweries come under the umbrella of New Zealand
Breweries: Canterbury Brewery (see page 110), Speight's (see
page 123) and Lion Breweries, in Newmarket. The Great
Northern Brewery, as Lion Breweries was first called, was
established in 1860 over a spring in Newmarket by Richard
Seccombe, who used the lion from his family crest on the logo.
Lion Breweries was established after a merger between the
Great Northern and Albert breweries in 1915, and in 1958 a
modern brewing plant was built on the current site. The
brewery is New Zealand's largest, with a capacity of 140 million
litres per year. A number of Lion products are brewed and
packaged in Newmarket for local and overseas markets.

Ice 4.7% abv

A very pale straw colour, Ice beer has a fruity, sweet aroma. It is very
light in texture, clean and smooth. Designed for uncomplicated, easy
drinking, its flavour is also relatively sweet and floral with a short
finish. Ice is a beer in the modern style, aimed at the drinker looking
for a light, quaffing beverage, and it numbers amongst its fans many
who do not consider themselves beer drinkers. The subtle flavour is
good for any simple seafood dish, but it is also an ideal contrast to
hot and spicy Indian curries, calming the palate.

Light Ice 2.5% abv

Light Ice is a low-alcohol beer that is pale straw in colour with a
distinctively floral and fruity aroma. The crisp texture and very little

mouth-feel give it a refreshing quality. The flavour is full, sweet and floral with a little spiciness at the end. There is some mild hop flavour present that adds weight. It is a complement to spicy ethnic foods or a safe bet on its own.

Lion Red 4% abv

For a long time New Zealand's biggest-selling beer, Lion Red more or less defines the Kiwi brown-beer style. It is mid-brown in colour and has a smooth, mouth-filling texture. The aroma is malty with some evidence of fruit, while the flavour is full of malt sweetness balanced by a pleasant moderate hop bitterness. It has a good length and a mild aftertaste. This is a hugely popular beer best served fresh and enjoyed with any red-meat dish — its robust maltiness is a good match with the full flavour of a rich, hearty casserole.

Rheineck Lager 4% abv

Its name may sound German, but Rheineck has a long Kiwi heritage. Born at the now-closed Waikato Breweries in Hamilton, this lager-style beer is light tan-gold in colour and has a malt fruit aroma. The texture is slightly creamy and it is smooth and with good body. The hop character is understated on the palate and its sweetish, malty character is more dominant — overall it is a 'softer' beer for those who like the rounder finish. Rheineck makes a subtle companion to a variety of spicy dishes, particularly complex south-east Asian cuisine like satay prawns.

Waikato Draught 4% abv

A persistent favourite, Waikato Draught is golden brown in colour with a complex, fruity, hoppy and spicy aroma. The texture is once again smooth and clean and the mouth-feel is generous. The taste is comparatively strong, with malt and hop each contributing flavour.

There is an element of bitterness to Waikato that carries the flavour into a robust finish. This means it is a good match for a hearty meat-and-potatoes meal and without doubt that piece of sirloin just off the barbecue.

Lion Brown 4% abv

Rich copper-brown is the colour of this beer so very popular in the lower North Island. It has a malty aroma with some hop offering freshly mown grass characteristics. It is full-bodied and mouth-filling in texture — almost creamy. On the palate there is hop flavour evident as well as a hint of sweetness and a nutty, biscuity note If you are looking for floral or winey characters, you will be disappointed. It's ideal for that rack of lamb.

Steinlager 5% abv

An icon on the New Zealand beer scene, Steinlager has many supporters, especially those who like a hoppier tipple. It is light brown with a slight lime hue in the glass. The aroma is dry with plenty of hops evident, and some hay and garden-herb characters come through as well. Steinlager is full flavoured with plenty of mouth-feel, a distinctive grassy note and a dry, astringent finish. It is a challenging beer for some but offers a real alternative to the ubiquitous sweet Kiwi brown-beer style. Steinlager complements any dish that includes herbs, particularly Mediterranean food. Try it with rare smoked beef with a sun-dried tomato pesto.

Leopard Black Label 4.5% abv

Another golden brown beer in the lager style, this offering has an aroma rich in malt fruit with some hop character as well as a slight biscuity note. The texture is crisp and clean with good mouth-feel and plenty of length. The flavour reminds me of light fruitcake with a suggestion of caramel, sweet rather than bitter — although some will find a certain bitterness as well. It is a well-balanced beer with a refreshingly distinctive character that comes from the type of yeast used. Serve it up next time you have paua fritters or, for something different, moussaka.

Galbraith Brewing Company

ADDRESS 2 Mount Eden Road, Mount Eden, Auckland **PHONE** (09) 379 3557 **FAX** (09) 307 6721 **E-MAIL** brewaben@ihug.co.nz **BREWER** Keith Galbraith **OPEN** noon–11 pm Sun–Wed, 11 am– midnight Thu–Sat

Galbraith's Ale House opened in June 1995 and has been developing a constantly expanding coterie of devotees ever since. Only English-style 'real ales' are brewed and served on site and the attention to detail in pursuit of authenticity is amazing. All are top-fermented, unfiltered and unpasteurised, and are cask conditioned to boot. They are served without carbonation straight from the conditioning casks by hand pump at a cellar temperature of 10–12°C. The result is a range of beer that is full and strong and ideal for savouring. Keith Galbraith is a true innovator in the New Zealand craft brewing context and the Ale House is testimony to the passion and effort he puts into his craft. The beer and a full menu are available at the Ale House.

Bob Hudson's Bitter 4% abv

Rose-gold with a thick creamy head, this bitter has delightful aromatics: citrus and honey with full malt and lashings of tropical fruit, mango and banana influences. The texture is rich and creamy and the flavour is complex with sweet and floral characters sitting easily with plenty of hop bitterness and bite. It is an easy-drinking ale sure to please those with a preference for the hop. Antipasto would bring out the complexity of this beer; for a simpler option try grilled pork chops with a touch of apple sauce.

Bellringers Bitter 4.5% abv

A burnished copper, almost amber colour and a creamy white head characterise this beer named after a group of regular customers. There are ripe berryfruit influences in the aroma, together with chocolate-malt notes. The texture is creamy, the mouth-feel full and fresh. A well-balanced blend of malt sweetness and hop bitterness best describes the flavour, which is probably why this beer is the biggest seller across the Galbraith's bar. I'd serve it in true English fashion — with classic toad-in-the-hole.

Grafton Porter 5% abv

'A full-bodied dark ale' is how Keith describes this beer, which seems an accurate way to summarise its almost black colour and full, creamy texture. The aroma is mild, with a little coffee and caramel in the bouquet. The use of roasted and chocolate malts without doubt provides the basis of its lovely malty flavour, which lingers long and strong. Hop lovers should have no fear — the bitterness is there to keep the balance. Try it with a selection of cheese for a long summer lunch, or a rich stout and stilton soup by the fireside.

Bitter and Twisted 5.3% abv

This is my favourite of Keith Galbraith's range of quite exceptional beers. Mid-amber in colour with a malt fruit and tobacco aroma, a smooth, creamy texture and a generous, well-balanced flavour profile, this beer can be enjoyed at any time of day or year. The quality of the ingredients shines through, each being allowed to stand on its merits while contributing wonderfully to the whole. It has everything I seek in a beer: aromatics, texture and body, balanced flavours and plenty of character to keep me interested. The high alcohol content means it is a great palate stimulator, but if seeking a menu partner I'd opt for quail, roasted in a stout berryfruit sauce and served with a selection of root vegetables.

Australis Brewing Company

ADDRESS 2 Mount Eden Road, Mount Eden, Auckland **PHONE** (09) 379 3557 **FAX** (09) 307 6721 **E-MAIL** brewaben@ihug.co.nz **BREWERS** Keith Galbraith & Ben Middlemass

Australis Brewing Company was set up by Keith Galbraith and Ben Middlemass in 1998 to produce high-quality, bottle-conditioned beer for more adventurous beer palates. Under this label the pair will brew traditional beer styles, some of which have been almost lost over time. The vintage-dated beers are primarily designed for the table, not as barbecue quaffers. They are sold over the counter at Galbraith's Ale House or as packaged products via mail order. While not cheap, these fuller-strength ales are of a style of beer not found elsewhere in New Zealand and are well worth trying if you hanker for something at the opposite end of the scale from the typical Kiwi brown ale.

Benediction Belgian Abbey-Style Ale 8.7% abv
The rich, spicy-fruit, slightly astringent aroma of this beer is still powerful as it rises through a thick, creamy head from an ale that is a deep golden-tan colour. The texture is creamy, the mouth-feel full

and luscious. The flavour is extravagant with influences of malt and cloves with a full hop kick in the lingering finish: one mouthful and you know you are supping a very fine, very strong ale. It is perfect as an aperitif or savoured with a generous cut of finest sirloin, served rare and seasoned with a blue-cheese sauce.

Romanov Baltic Stout 7.8% abv

Dark brown, almost black in colour, Romanov Baltic Stout has an incredible aroma of roasted malt and Marmite with a hint of yeast. It is rich and creamy with a concentrated bitter-sweet flavour — a blend of fruit and hops that is big and bold and demands attention. The finish is glorious and simply lingers and lingers. Complement this excellent example of the style with a dozen of the finest fresh oysters you can buy. Serve them *au naturel*.

Hodgson India Pale Ale 6.3% abv

Slightly lighter than its fellow beers, the IPA is tan rather than brown. Its aroma is full of malt with hints of orange peel, honey and spice resulting in a perfumed, almost floral, bouquet. Soft and velvety is the best way to describe the texture, while the mouth-feel is robust and lingering. It fair bursts with intense flavours, a balance of malt and hop, the quality and generosity of ingredients shining through. It is a beer for the most discerning drinker, and a partner for the most stylish meal. Serve with wild venison shanks in a hotpot of smoked sausage, duck, sweet potato and roast pumpkin.

FACT Beer writers have uncovered an old beer recipe for Cock Ale that calls for a rooster to be placed in a bag and put into the mash, presumably to add body and character.

Trident Tavern

ADDRESS 69 Selwyn Street, Onehunga, Auckland **PHONE** (09) 636 9070
FAX (09) 622 0764 **BREWER** John Duke **OPEN** 10 am–11 pm Mon–
Wed, 10 am–1 am Thu–Sat; lounge bar open 11 am–8.30 pm Sun

The Trident Tavern is a reasonably large, established complex
in the Auckland suburb of Onehunga. As well as a number of
bars, it has a well-patronised liquor store and, uncommonly
for this style of operation, a small brewery. The brewery
supplies the hotel and patrons who want to take beer home.
Owned by the entrepreneurial Sel and Ivy Bennett, the Trident
Tavern is the meeting place for a host of locals who come to
enjoy the camaraderie and the atmosphere. The beers are
mainstream and obviously appeal to the many patrons, each
of whom has his or her clear favourite. The selection is wide
and varied, with some common brewing themes running
through.

Sel's Pub Lager 4% abv

A pale gold colour and a very mild malt aroma form the first
impressions of this session lager. The texture is lightweight with little
mouth-feel and a short finish. There is some malt influence in the
flavour, along with some citrus character, but it is a dryness that
may come from the hops that is the most obvious feature. On the
day this felt like a very young beer, which may explain its texture
and dryness. It would be difficult to match it with a food that didn't
overwhelm it — fish is probably best.

Sel's Pub Draft 4% abv

This beer is the colour of golden syrup — a deep golden brown. The
aroma reminds me of the inside of a freezer, while the texture is

light and clean. There are some light malt flavours as well as a little hop character. This is a particularly dry, brown quaffing beer with a short finish suitable for serving at a barbecue or around a camp fire.

Sel's Ice Beer 4% abv

Another pale gold offering, this one has a distinct apple-cider aroma. There is medium mouth-feel and a lightweight texture to carry the flavour. The predominant taste is the malt, which is most likely responsible for the residual sweetness. In this beer the hop influence is more pronounced and so is the dryness/bitterness that characterises many of the Trident brews. This is a good summer session beer best served with beef and garlic sausages hot off the grill.

Sel's Super 4% abv

This is my pick of the Trident brews. It is gold with a lime hue and an aroma of tropical fruit with some spiciness. The texture is crisp and clean. It has medium mouth-feel and good length. The balance between malt and hop is welcome and there is a hint of caramel in the flavour to keep it interesting. There is a degree of hop bitterness on the back palate, giving this beer a 'drink me' character. Partner it with spicy tortillas or any other dish that has some fire to it.

Sel's Pub Dark 4% abv

The Pub Dark is actually a reddish brown colour. While there is no aroma to speak of, the texture is creamy and smooth, typical of the style. It has a mild flavour combining some roasted malt character with a bit of coffee and some toffee to boot. Another offering with some residual hop bitterness resulting in an extended length of flavour, it is more a Kiwi brown beer than a dark beer, but all the same it's a welcome variation in the Trident range. Save it for the hearty meat-pie occasion.

Onehunga Spring Brewery

ADDRESS 2 Miami Parade, Onehunga, Auckland **PHONE** (09) 834 1890 **FAX** (09) 834 1520 **E-MAIL** ian.ramsay@clear.net.nz **BREWER** Ian Ramsay **OPEN** 10 am–5.30 pm Mon–Fri, 10 am–2 pm Sat & Sun

Onehunga Spring Brewery has been on its suburban Auckland site for twelve years. Owner Carl Wackrow says his goal is to batch-brew quality New Zealand-style beers with no added sugars, appealing to those who appreciate the boutique brewery style. Onehunga Spring beers have won medals at the Australasian Beer Awards and are available from the brewery and most major retail liquor outlets in Auckland as packaged product. An interesting point of difference about Onehunga Spring is its willingness to contract-brew in small or large quantities; for a small charge Carl and his team can organise personalised labels.

Silver Fern New Zealand Lager 4% abv

A pale straw colour with a slight lime tinge and a generous white head announce the aroma, which is distinctively hops, leather and hay, balanced with a bit of tropical fruit. The texture is crisp and clean, the flavour hoppy at the front of the palate, sweeter on the back. The flavour quickly disappears, resulting in no great length. Silver Fern is a mild quaffer, great to accompany a bowl of Mexican chilli.

Old Thumper Robust Malt Beer 4% abv

In the glass Old Thumper is a dark gold colour. The aroma is a blend of malt and Marmite, the texture light with good mouth-feel and a fairly lengthy finish. Coffee and malt flavours dominate, giving the beer a Christmas-fruit character balanced by medium hop bitterness.

It is a full-flavoured beer that perhaps is a little light in texture and in need of some extra alcohol. It would be good with game meat or with roast quail.

Spring Brewery Natural Lager 4% abv

This lager is, like its sister brew, a pale straw colour. However the aroma is different, this one having honey and citrus characters that are stronger than the malt fruit notes that you can also pick up. In the mouth it is very light and with no length. The flavour is mild too, with just a hint of malt sweetness and even milder hop bitterness. I suggest you match this one up with fish — perhaps hoki or snapper with a lemon butter sauce.

Spring Natural Red Ale 4% abv

Golden yellow in colour, this beer has a mildly musty aroma with some cooked vegetable character. The body is smooth and creamy, the flavour wheaty with some honey influences. The sweetness of this beer will account for its appeal as a mainstream quaffer best paired with simple food, perhaps sausages off the barbecue.

Spring Brewery Natural Draught 4% abv

An interesting shade of copper-gold, this beer has an aroma that suggests malt, tropical fruit and caramel. The texture is crisp and clean with a certain freshness about it. The toasted malts used in its production account for the coffee and chocolate flavours. It is a nicely balanced beer, easy to drink and very good as a food beer. Mussels in garlic would be my pick as a match.

Old Black Strong Winter Stout 6% abv

As you would expect, this is a very dark brown beer, with hints of toffee, malt fruit and caramel making up the aroma. The texture is creamy and smooth with a generous mouth-feel that lingers. The flavour is of malt and dark chocolate, with almost a molasses character. There is not too much hop influence, rather a pleasant sweetness on the back palate. This is a beer sure to please those who appreciate the higher-strength and fuller-flavour offerings. Remember carpetbag steaks? This beer is a good excuse to resurrect the recipe.

Waitemata Brewery (DB Breweries)

ADDRESS Cnr Bairds & Great South Roads, Otahuhu, Auckland **PHONE** (09) 276 3875 **FAX** (09) 276 8475 **WEBSITE** www.dbbreweries.co.nz **BREWER** Phil Murray **TOURS** 10.30 am Tue–Fri

DB Breweries, part of DB Group Ltd, maintains four breweries at Waitemata, Mangatainoka (Tui Brewery, see page 73), Greymouth (Monteith's Brewing Company, see page 101) and Timaru (Mainland Brewery, see page 116). Brewer William Coutts opened the original Waitemata Brewery in Auckland in 1930. In the period following World War II the brewery underwent considerable expansion. In 1950 Coutts's son Morton began research on the continuous-fermentation method of brewing. This replaced the previously used batch system, allowing a flow of ingredients in the fermentation. In 1988 DB Breweries became part of Magnum Corporation, one of two major New Zealand liquor and food distribution corporations. In late 1992 Magnum was renamed DB Group. The company is a major supporter of a variety of community, sporting and cultural activities around New Zealand. DB beers are available as packaged product and on tap from bars, restaurants and retail liquor stores throughout the country.

DB Bitter 4% abv

DB Bitter is a full-flavoured mainstream bitter beer. It has a malt fruit aroma with a hint of grain and grassiness. The texture is crisp and clean and the flavour has a good balance of malt sweetness and hop. It's an easy-to-drink session beer with good mouth-feel and a moderately bitter finish. This is a perfect beer for everyday dishes at home or when eating out with mates. Serve it with curried sausages.

DB Export Dry 5% abv

This beer has a golden grain colour and a cut-grass and tropical-fruit aroma. It has good mouth-feel and a crisp texture that gives the impression of freshness. The flavour, too, is crisp and somewhat dry, with mild hop influences and evidence of fruit. On the finish there is a residual sweetness that, together with another hint of hop, provides welcome length. This award-winning beer is an ideal accompaniment when experimenting with adventurous cuisines, perfect to cool the palate after forays into the spices of the orient and the Middle East. Go for curry or for spicy lamb kebabs!

DB Natural 4% abv

Judged the world's best ale at an international competition in 1994, DB Natural is a pale gold beer with a distinctive hop aroma tinged with some yeasty notes. It is light in texture, clean and crisp, with a full-bodied mouth-feel. Hop characters and some familiar sweetness dominate the palate and there is some grassy, haybarn character as well. This popular beer matches well with seafood, pasta and white meats cooked on the barbecue.

Export Gold 4% abv

Export Gold is a deep golden, full-strength lager with a fresh mild hop and malt aroma. On the palate it is refreshing and smooth with good mouth-filling qualities. The flavour is moderately malty with some pleasant biscuity influences and it has a well-balanced, lengthy finish. This is a premium lager beer that, like most lagers, is ideal for pairing with spicy ethnic cuisines such as Thai, Indonesian and Indian.

Heineken 5% abv

Heineken is brewed by DB Breweries in New Zealand under licence. Strict quality control ensures that the features which make this a universally admired brew are matched in the local version. A mid-gold colour with a slight lime tinge, Heineken has a hoppy aroma with some freshly milled grain character. The texture is rich and smooth, the flavour full with a slightly fruity yet mildly bitter taste, and there is a good level of effervescence. It has a wonderful length with a welcome hop bitterness of moderate strength. It is a great accompaniment to shellfish, light chicken dishes and herb-influenced pasta. Try it with seafood linguine!

Super Dry 5% abv

Super Dry has a light brown colour and a fresh fruit and malt aroma tinged with a hint of grain. The texture is light and refreshing with a crisp finish. It has a slightly floral, fruity flavour with a very mild hop influence. It's not overtly dry but the reduced sugar is noticeable on the back palate. It will complement seafood or chicken dishes — choose chicken with a Middle Eastern influence.

DB Natural Light 2.5% abv

DB Natural Light uses a unique brewing process that 'filters' the alcohol from the beer whilst retaining the flavour of a standard lager. It's light gold in colour with a very mild aroma. It has good body and appealing mouth-feel, and is smooth and clean with a surprising level of flavour and a pleasant aftertaste. It is well balanced and a find for those looking for a low-alcohol alternative. It will complement a wide range of food but, like most lagers, it goes best with seafood, chicken, oriental dishes and vegetarian food. Try it with blinis filled with salmon in a dill mayonnaise.

Flame Beer 5.2% abv

This beer was originally produced by Black Dog Brewery, one of DB Breweries' marketing inventions. It has a very loyal following, especially in the urban café and club scene. It is a vivid amber-brown in colour with a moderately floral, sweet fruit aroma. It is crisp and clean and best drunk quite cold. The flavour has elements of honey and tropical fruit with enough bite to keep it refreshing. While it has moderate length, there is plenty of flavour on the back palate. It's best enjoyed as a quaffer on the big night out.

Auckland Breweries

ADDRESS 186 James Fletcher Drive, Otahuhu, Auckland **PHONE** (09) 270 1890 **FAX** (09) 270 1893 **BREWER** Nigel Shaw

Auckland Breweries is a comparative newcomer to the Auckland brewing scene. The privately owned operation opened in late 1997 with a shareholding mix of some people associated with the sale of beer and some who are not. The company objective is to brew a range of price-competitive, mainstream products that compete with those of the major breweries. Auckland Breweries has a large brewing capacity and currently supplies keg product to clubs and pubs throughout the North Island. A special range, Charters, is brewed for the Chartered Club network. There are plans to begin packaging Auckland Breweries products for retail sale in the near future.

Auckland Lager 4% abv

Straw coloured and highly carbonated, this lager style has a mild malt and hop aroma and a crisp and clean texture. The flavour is sweet with honey and citrus characteristics prevailing, a short finish and overall a refreshing quality. It is a beer typical of its style and so appeals to those who prefer mild flavours and have no hankering for hops. Take a few when eating Mexican or some other fiery ethnic fare.

Auckland Draught 4% abv

A bright gold in colour with a thick, creamy head, this beer has a neutral aroma with slight grassiness when it warms to room temperature. The texture is smooth and clean with lightweight mouth-feel. It's an easy-to-drink offering with a malty, sweet flavour and a touch of yeastiness about it. It's a summer quaffer to enjoy with your favourite barbecue food or as an accompaniment to cottage pie.

Auckland Dark 4% abv

Dark amber-brown best describes the colour of this beer, which also has an appealing, thick, creamy head. There is plenty of malt and molasses in the bouquet, while the texture is light and creamy with good mouth-feel and a short finish. The flavour is full of fruit sweetness with a hint of coffee and molasses, milder than some made in this style. It's a fairly lightweight example of a dark beer, perfect for those new to the style, and overall it makes pleasant drinking. Serve it with any tasty roast or, for a special treat, raw oysters.

> **FACT** In 1740 Admiral Vernon of the British fleet decided to water down the navy's rum. Needless to say, the sailors weren't too pleased and called Admiral Vernon 'Old Grog', after the stiff wool grogram coats he wore. The term 'grog' soon began to mean the watered-down drink itself. When you were drunk on this grog, you were 'groggy'.

Tarawera Draught 4% abv

Tarawera Draught is copper-gold and once again has a malty, sweet aroma with some sign of chocolate and hops on the nose. The texture is clean and smooth, not as crisp as the Auckland Draught. The roasted malt characters come through on the palate, as does the hop bitterness that, while mild in intensity, adds a welcome depth. A mainstream draught beer appealing to a wide spectrum of Kiwi beer drinkers, it will be at home on most dinner tables — especially when grilled pork chops are on the menu.

Steam Brewing Company

ADDRESS 272 Ti Rakau Drive, East Tamaki, Auckland **PHONE** (09) 273 7012 **FAX** (09) 273 7246 **E-MAIL** kieran@ihug.co.nz **BREWER** Luke Nicholas **OPEN** 11.30 am–late daily

The Cock & Bull English Pub is in the eastern suburbs of Auckland. Part of the complex, opened in 1995, is a fully operational brewery under the guiding hand of enthusiastic young brewer Luke Nicholas, who is instrumental in promoting the interests of New Zealand craft brewers. A full menu is available for lunch and dinner and there is also a function room for hire. Luke, with the support of Cock & Bull owner Kieran Meyer, brews to satisfy customer preferences but at the same time seeks to develop broader interest in beer by offering a selection of new styles and seasonal beers. The brewery's beers have won many awards and continue to delight a large and very loyal band of customers who travel from near and far to enjoy the beer and the atmosphere of the Cock & Bull.

Cock & Bull Lager 4.3% abv

A bright tan-gold in colour, this beer has an aroma that is full of malt, with some toffee and some banana influences as well. There is also a faint suggestion of mealiness. The texture is crisp and clean, while the flavour is soft with a good balance of malt and hop. It is dry around the palate with some honey character towards the back. Rich and flavourful, with plenty of length, it is a good food beer worth going to some effort to match. Try it with lasagne!

Classic Draft 3.8% abv

This is another golden beer, with a very mild aroma of malt fruit and a light and smooth texture. There is a pleasant mouth-feel that makes it fit comfortably into the mainstream category, although it's a class or two above the average in terms of balance and flavour. There are some fruit characters evident on the palate and the hops make a contribution to the flavour. It has good length. All in all, this is a fine, full-flavoured session beer. Try serving it with barbecued calamari.

Fuggles Best Bitter 4.5% abv

One of two hand-pulled beers at the Cock & Bull, this golden brown beer has a lovely cascade when poured and a generous, creamy head. It has an interesting aroma of sherbet and fruit with some rose petal, almost floral character as well. The texture is slightly spritzy but at the same time soft and creamy with great mouth-filling qualities. The flavour is mildly malty at first — and then you get real bitter herb tastes as well. This intense bitterness lasts and lasts but is never biting on the back palate. True to style, it is a favourite with the hop lovers. I'd have it with lamb chops and mint sauce.

Hop Head Pale Ale 4.2% abv

This American-style pale ale is mid-tan in colour and has a sweet honey and fruit aroma with some hoppiness. The texture is crisp and fresh, leaving an impression of balance with good mouth-feel. The flavour is very hoppy from start to finish, hence the name. The hops also impart their characteristic bitterness, giving the beer good length and a pleasant dryness — creating an appeal for more. If hop influence is your preference here is another beer sure to please. It will go well with any dishes that have a herbaceous element: enjoy it with chorizo and a potato and thyme mash.

Monks Habit

Supreme champion

The brewer is a bit coy about the alcohol content of this beer, but there is no doubt it is a fuller-strength offering. A rich golden brown in colour, it has a full malt fruit aroma with some Christmas-cake character as well. On the palate it is creamy and smooth with wonderful mouth-feel. The flavour is well balanced, with sweetish malt and fruit on the front and hop flavour on the sides and back, and hop bitterness providing the length. After a couple of mouthfuls you also taste soft honey and caramel influences as well. A favourite of mine, it is wonderful as an aperitif. It's equally good when you use its full flavour to match a hearty roast of beef with a rich, dark gravy.

Dark Star 4% abv

Very dark brown, almost black in colour, Dark Star has lots of caramel and coffee with some biscuit characters in the aroma. The texture is light and smooth with a medium level of creaminess. The taste is medium-sweet with roasted malt and some chocolate and caramel flavours coming through. There is excellent mouth-feel with this beer, even though it doesn't have a long finish. It is in the style of a porter and I would serve it with blue cheese or even a good-quality aged cheddar.

Independent Brewery

ADDRESS 35 Hunua Road, Papakura, Auckland **PHONE** (09) 298 3000 **FAX** (09) 299 6699 **BREWER** Tony Denny

Independent Brewery, New Zealand's third largest brewery, is a subsidiary of the privately owned Independent Liquor. It produces a number of beers for export and has two products for the local market that are distributed primarily through privately owned liquor stores throughout the country. The company claims that with these two products they have about ten per cent of the local canned-beer market. The Independent Brewery philosophy is to brew mainstream, price-competitive beers that provide a direct alternative to the two major breweries. The philosophy also includes selling only fresh product, and the brewery will store the beer for only four to five days after packaging before shipping it to customers.

New Zealand Lager 5% abv

A bright yellow-gold colour makes this an attractive beer in the glass. It has a complex aroma, with hints of apple cider, malt, yeast, hops and a mild sweetness all having an influence. The texture is moderately creamy, clean with plenty of mouth-feel. A balance of malt sweetness and hop flavour comes through on the palate, with some grassiness, herb and hay notes also making an appearance. It has good length and is, overall, a very good example of the Kiwi lager style. For a food match I would serve pan-fried fish with tomatoes, spring onions and a touch of garlic.

Ranfurly Draught 4% abv

The colour of this beer is orange-gold and it has a thick, creamy head that lingers. There are touches of tropical fruit and malt as well as yeast in the aroma, while the texture is light and creamy with a generous mouth-feel. It has a mild malt flavour as well as some caramel and toffee influences. On the back palate there is some astringency that offsets the residual sweetness. It is a pleasant, easy-drinking brown beer with a good length. This is an ideal red-meat partner, and I would try it with Lancashire hotpot.

Kahikatea Brewery

ADDRESS 258 Kahikatea Drive, Hamilton **PHONE** (07) 847 0705 **FAX** (07) 847 0706 **BREWER** Gordon Cadman **OPEN** 9 am–6 pm Mon–Sat; free tasting on Sat

Kahikatea Brewery, established in 1995, makes the only locally produced beer in the Hamilton area. The brewer from the original Waikato Brewery, Brian Ronson, and his partners decided they would revive the original Waikato style and produce high-quality, batch-brewed, full-malt beers. Today, under the guiding hand of brewer Gordon Cadman and using 100 per cent barley malt, Kahikatea Brewery offers beverages for the mainstream consumer. The beer is distributed to clubs and pubs in the Waikato and Coromandel areas, where it has a very loyal following. It is available directly from the brewery or from selected outlets throughout the district.

Kahikatea Cold Gold 5% abv

This beer has a pale straw colour and a pronounced hop aroma arising from the predominant use of the Green Bullet hop. The texture is as you would expect from a lager style — crisp and clean, the mouth-feel most luscious on the middle palate. The hop influence is more subtle when it comes to flavour and the malt sweetness has the upper hand. Best enjoyed very cold, this easy-to-drink, uncomplicated quaffer should go best with spicy food in the summer months and with a good hot Thai curry any time.

Kahikatea Draught 4% abv

The first thing you notice about this mid-straw-coloured beer is the mass of bubbles that indicates its high level of carbonation. The aroma is appealing, with cut-grass and citrus influences coming to the fore and a tanginess that derives from the Saaz hops favoured by the brewer. A little unusual for its style, this is a creamy beer with a very short finish. It is slightly mealy on the palate, with some hop bitterness aided and abetted by some sweetness, probably from the malt. While not dry, this beer has good cut-through, which means it will partner creamy or rich food well — try it with fettuccine.

Kahikatea Dark Ale 4% abv

Rather than jet black, this beer is more mid-dark with a slight red tinge. There is an obvious malt aroma with some cocoa too. The texture is slightly creamy without the harshness on the back palate common in dark beers. I picked up flavours of malt fruitiness, some caramel, cocoa again and a mealiness from the roasted barley used in the brewing process. A popular option with the locals, this is a light, eminently drinkable example of the style. Try it with golden syrup steamed pudding or a fruit mince tart.

Kahikatea Best Bitter 4% abv

Red-gold in colour with a very slight, soft aroma of malt sweetness, this beer is one for those who enjoy caramel/coffee flavours. There is also a touch of almond for the very sensitive palate and a reasonable level of hop bitterness. The mouth-feel is generous with a shortish finish. It is a quaffer to be enjoyed with red-meat dishes, perhaps corned beef cooked with a few cloves, brown sugar and a whole onion.

Sunshine Brewing Company

ADDRESS 109 Disraeli Street, Gisborne **PHONE** (06) 867 7777 **FAX** (06) 867 1141 **BREWERS** Geoff Logan & Gerry Maude **OPEN** 9 am– 6 pm Mon–Sat

Sunshine is a little brewery with a large reputation, especially in the Gisborne region where locals flock to fill up with their favourite from the interesting range of mainstream beers presented at competitive prices. Brewers Geoff Logan and Gerry Maude are engaging personalities, eager to satisfy the most discerning drinker, and if time between brews permits they are happy to discuss with customers their abiding passion — beer. Sunshine Brewing Company beers have won numerous awards. They can be purchased from the brewery itself and can be found on tap in selected pubs in the North Island, particularly in the Wellington region.

Gisborne Gold 4% abv

Yellow-gold with a light hop aroma, this is perhaps Geoff's most mainstream beer. Appealing to the lager drinker, it has a good hop/malt balance and is nicely dry with good length. While not full of flavour, it has a hint of hazelnut that adds character and interest. It would be good with spicy food or simply as a summer thirst quencher.

Gisborne Bitter 4% abv

Rich honey-gold with a slight hop aroma, this beer has a deceptively creamy texture with a nuttiness and a lingering bitterness across the palate. It is a good, balanced beer ideal for those looking for a light ale with a kick in the tail. I am going to try it next with a smoked-chicken and pinenut salad.

Sundowner Dark Ale 4.5% abv

This dark amber-brown beer has Black Magic added to it to make a 50/50 blend. It is big and mouth-filling with plenty of chocolate and nut flavours and a nice, gentle hop bitterness. Rich and malty with a hint of Vegemite, it is my favourite from this brewery and would be great as an aperitif or as a partner to a hearty roast with rich gravy.

Moonshine Strong Pilsener 6.5% abv

Pale straw in colour, this beer has a high hop aroma and a hop bitterness to match. The taste reminds me a little of vermouth and it has the same dryness about it. There is also a nice touch of tropical

---

FACT The first purity laws date from the Babylonian lawgiver Hammurabi's time 4000 years ago and condemn brewers who make bad beer to be thrown into the river.

fruit to provide balance. A beer for the true hop-head, it is worth trying with a tomato and basil pasta. Or get daring and serve it with cheese flavoured with cumin seed.

Black Magic 5% abv

This stout is very black with a slightly grainy texture and strong malt/molasses notes in the aroma. It doesn't have the length you might expect — instead it is light and refreshing and full of flavour, with hints of coffee and cooking chocolate. I would partner it with steak off the barbecue or even a chocolate mousse!

Brew Haus

ADDRESS Club Habitat, 25 Ohuanga Rd, Turangi **PHONE** (07) 386 7492 **FAX** (07) 386 0106 **BREWER** Hamish Betteridge **OPEN** 5 pm–late daily

Turangi's Club Habitat offers visitors to the central North Island — skiers, backpackers, conference groups and anyone else looking for lodgings — a variety of accommodation options and a full *à la carte* menu if required. An added attraction and a great drawcard is the brewery situated between the restaurant and the bar, where diners and bar patrons can see the beer being made. The brewery is a compact little number, one of several Canadian imports now in use around the country. It is an impressive sight when there is a brew being put down, and the aroma wafting around the complex is delicious. Brewer Hamish Betteridge knows how to satisfy his regular local customers, but he is at his happiest when indulging his passion for creating brews for the more adventurous beer taster. The full range is available on site.

Brew Haus Lager 4% abv

Pale straw in colour with a slight green hue, this lager has a distinct hop aroma — not too strident, not too light. The brewer's use of Saaz hops seems appropriate, giving lovely balanced lager characteristics. It is clean and crisp, with reasonably subtle flavours and a good, lingering bitterness. A favourite with the regulars, it is uncomplicated and will go down well either on its own or with a selection of continental sausage — salami, bratwurst, etc.

Brew Haus Malt Ale 4% abv

The ale is amber coloured and produces a thick, creamy head. The aroma is malty and sweet with a hint of fruit mince. The texture is clean and there is plenty of body, although not a huge finish. The flavour is of chocolate and caramel with a touch of sweet coffee. A nicely rounded beer that would benefit from a little more bitterness, it would be easy to enjoy with a winter roast.

Brew Haus Pilsener 5.2% abv

A light straw in colour, this beer has the most complex aroma of the range. Both malt and hop characters are present, as is a honey sweetness. The texture is crisp and clean and there is plenty of length. The flavour is well rounded, with some sweetness and a touch of hop bitterness around the edges of the tongue. The higher alcohol content adds a welcome kick, but this lager style still fits into the mainstream category. It would be good with spicy food — chicken satay springs to mind.

Brew Haus Dark Ale 4% abv

This is a striking beer in the glass, with a real amber hue to it. The first whiffs are of caramel and malt. The beer is full bodied and rich yet is better described as a light ale. The flavour reflects the chocolate malt used without the overpowering burnt-coffee characteristic that mars so many other dark beers. It is easy to drink, without much lingering flavour. Red-meat dishes will go well but the daring may like to try a smoky cheese.

Brew Haus Weiss Beer 4.8% abv

A soft straw colour, this brew is a little cloudy in the wheat-beer style. The aroma is of papaya and cloves — others detect banana fritters as well. There are some delicious tropical-fruit flavours that match the nose. There is also a little spiciness on the back palate. The texture is smooth and creamy and there is plenty of length to provide lingering enjoyment. It's not everybody's preferred style but is well worth trying. It is great as an aperitif but I would serve it with apple shortcake.

White Cliffs Brewing Company

ADDRESS Main Road North (SH 3), Urenui, Taranaki **PHONE & FAX** (06) 752 3676 **E-MAIL** mikes@brewing.co.nz **BREWER** Mike Johnson **OPEN** 9.30 am–6 pm Mon–Sat

In September 1989 unemployed Taranaki man Mike Johnson decided to expand his home-brew experience by opening White Cliffs Brewing Company at Urenui, on the west coast of the North Island. By 1998 White Cliffs was brewing 45,000 litres of Mike's Pale Ale per year and had rated a huge mention in Michael Jackson's highly acclaimed book *Beer*. Jackson rates it as a very good and 'rare example of a New World mild'. Packaged in riggers, stubbies and kegs, Mike's Mild is available in Taranaki, Taupo, Wellington, Queenstown, Nelson and Hamilton.

Mike's Mild Ale 4% abv

Amber-brown in colour, this unpasteurised and unfiltered beer has an appealing earthy, mushroomy aroma with a whiff of caramel adding sweetness. It has plenty of body and remains fresh and light from first to last. The flavour is mild on the tastebuds, biscuity and malty. It is complex and full and benefits from the addition of secondary hops fairly late in the process. It's a beer that, although technically a lager, will appeal to ale drinkers who have the good fortune to sample this true labour of love. It is good with mushroom fettuccine or a hearty beef hotpot.

O'Neills Brewing Company

ADDRESS 4281 Mountain Road, Ngaere, Stratford **PHONE** (06) 764 7209 **FAX** (06) 764 8313 **BREWERS** Helen & Brian O'Neill **OPEN** 11 am– 6 pm Mon–Thu, 11 am–late Fri & Sat **TOURS** by arrangement

On State Highway 3 between Stratford and Eltham in the Taranaki region you will find a tiny, blink-of-an-eye town called Ngaere. This is the home of a family-friendly bar and café that doubles as a brewery. Commissioned in 1996, it is a family business located in an old service station. O'Neills offers a selection of three beers in the bar and café. The beer is also available in pub pets from the brewery and from local bottle stores and clubs in Stratford.

O'Neills Black Peat 5% abv

Rather than the dark brown colour usual in the style, this beer is a deep amber-red. It is distinctly molasses/malt on the nose and the texture is medium in weight with a pleasing freshness. The flavour is typical: malty, dark chocolate, some candied fruit and residual hop bitterness on the back palate. It's an ideal choice next time you order fillet steak.

O'Neills Special Lager 4% abv

Mid-straw in colour, this beer has a mild aroma of citrus and hops. The texture is light, especially around the middle palate, and there is good length and a pleasant crispness. A combination of honey and cherry flavours is evident, along with a soft, malty aftertaste. An easy-to-drink quaffer good with food, it is probably best suited to some of the pizza available at O'Neills.

Egmont Pale Ale 4% abv

An interesting orange-tan in colour, this beer has no discernible aroma, although the sample I tried was very cold. It is very light and crisp in texture, while the flavour is of citrus with a slight smokiness. The beer has what I would call a wine character, with a real tang on the back palate that is not obviously hop driven. Not everyone's cup of tea, it is distinctive and individual. It's hard to recommend a food, but steer towards fish.

Coastal Breweries

ADDRESS 61 Main Road South, Manaia **PHONE & FAX** (06) 274 8240
BREWER Peter Taylor

Visitors to the tiny seaside town of Manaia, to the north of the Taranaki bight, may like to call in to the New Commercial Hotel. It is just across the road from Coastal Breweries and offers customers the freshest possible brew of Coastal Draught available. The brewery has been operating since 1996 and is the pride and joy of brewer Peter Taylor, who has plans to issue a number of other brews. In the meantime his offerings are popular with locals and can be purchased on tap or in flagons or bottles from the New Commercial. It is not currently available from the brewery.

Coastal Draught 4% abv

Tan-gold in colour with a slight cloudiness, this offering from Coastal Breweries has a sugary, malty aroma with a trace of chocolate. The flavour has some berryfruit character, some toffee and lots of coffee and chocolate. On the palate it wavers between dry and bitter, especially near the back of the throat. Although there are some signs of hop influence, it is the malt that predominates. Have it as an aperitif and even consider adding a little to the gravy for your Sunday roast.

Independent Brewery

ADDRESS 42 Holden Street, PO Box 3153, Onekawa, Napier **PHONE** (06) 843 3719 **FAX** (06) 843 2671 **BREWER** Tony Davies

The shareholders in the custom-built Independent Brewery have adopted a straight-up commercial philosophy. Their intention is to give their customers a no-frills alternative that competes on price and quality with the products of the larger breweries. This large wholesale beer manufacturer provides bulk beer to more than seventy-five outlets in the Central Plateau region and as far south as Wellington. Ninety per cent is sold under the Mates label from selected outlets, either in flagons or on tap, while others sell it under their own proprietary brand. It is available direct from the brewery only by prior arrangement.

Mates Gold 4% abv

The colour of this beer is best described as mid-straw. The rich aroma is heavy with bananas, butterscotch and tropical fruit. The texture is clean with a little stickiness and on the back palate it is slightly dry. It is light on flavour in the New Zealand light lager style and has only a very timid hop bitterness, almost a tartness, that many will find appealing. It is easy-drinking and will pair well with hot and spicy food such as barbecued chilli prawns.

Mates Amber 4% abv

Golden brown with lots of bubbles evident, this beer is light on aroma with only the merest hint of malt sweetness. It has a very smooth texture, making easy drinking at low temperature. This is not a highly flavoured beer and is clearly aimed at the Kiwi brown-beer drinker. It will go well with a lamb stew or cottage pie.

Mates Draught 4% abv

A slight orange-brown tint gives this beer immediate interest. On the nose it is reminiscent of fruit salad with a touch of molasses to boot. The texture is clean and very light with no real lasting impression. It is another typical New Zealand brown beer, low on hops and quite sweet with a barely discernible malt influence. Unchallenging and easy to drink, it is a good quaffer for the after-match function.

Mates Dark 4% abv

Like many similar beers this appears black but, held to the light, it is a very dark brown. It has a strong burnt-coffee aroma with hints of cooking chocolate. The texture is light — smooth but not creamy — while the flavour is typical caramel and molasses with a slight bitterness on the very back of the palate. The initial and middle impressions, however, are of sweet iced coffee. Savour it with a bit of wild venison or a pot roast and veges.

Roosters Brewhouse

ADDRESS 1470 Omahu Road, Hastings **PHONE** (06) 879 4127 **FAX** (06) 879 7410 **BREWERS** Chris O'Leary & Chris Harrison **OPEN** 10 am–7 pm Mon–Sat

Roosters Brewhouse is located on a busy stretch of highway between Napier and Hastings in Hawke's Bay. It's a relaxed and friendly place with a bar and beer garden, and a café serving casual meals. It offers an easy-going atmosphere where one can sit back inside or out and have a refreshing beer or two after a hot day in the Bay. The brewers cater to the tastebuds of more mainstream local patrons, but have also educated local palates to appreciate full-flavoured premium beers and beers of a not-so-common style. Roosters products are available in flagons from the brewery and from most liquor outlets in Hawke's Bay. They also have limited distribution in Wellington. Ask about the seasonal and occasional beers; every six weeks or so the guys produce special, hand-pulled beers ranging from pale ales to stouts.

Roosters Haymaker 7% abv
This powerful beer is pale straw in colour with a fruity aroma that brings to mind tinned pineapple. There are plenty of tropical-fruit flavours — pineapple dominates — as well as some malt sweetness. It has lots of body and a smooth lingering finish that fills the sinuses as well as the palate. Savour this as an aperitif — it certainly gets the appetite going.

Roosters Golden Wheat 4.3% abv

Very pale straw in colour with a lime tinge, this beer has a definite ginger and spice aroma that combines with a hint of grain dryness. There is enough sweetness to bring out the honey character and to provide a soft lingering finish. It is a good beer, one that I would serve with roast pork.

Roosters Draught 4% abv

This mainstream draught is dark gold in colour, with a very subtle aroma of malt. The texture is crisp and clean with plenty of body and length. The flavour is fruity — slightly citrusy, particularly orange. It is well balanced and makes pleasant drinking. Popular with locals, Roosters Draught will be enjoyable with a variety of meals — try it with shellfish to accommodate the citrus character.

Roosters Lager 5% abv

This is a yellow-gold lager style with a mild hop aroma infused with a little spiciness/pepperiness. Lightly flavoured and mildly hoppy, it has a surprising level of sweetness and a dryness that carries the enjoyment right to the back palate. The texture too is interesting in that it changes as the beer warms and goes from smooth throughout to clawing on the sides of the tongue. Choose food that will benefit from this beer's spiciness for maximum enjoyment, perhaps smoked fish pie.

Roosters Pale Blonde 5% abv

Made only occasionally, this brew is well worth trying. It's light yellow-gold in colour with a delicate aroma of the English hops used. The mild hoppiness comes through as the predominant flavour, although there is plenty of malt sweetness to balance it. To really enjoy this beer, drink it through the thick, creamy head. It's a meal in itself.

Roosters Dark Ale 5% abv

Dark amber-brown with wafting roast coffee and liquorice aromas, this beer has good body and is smooth and easy to drink. It has well-balanced chocolate/coffee flavours with another hint of that liquorice. A slight malt bitterness marks the finish of this beer and for some a certain nutty flavour makes an appearance. It is a pleasant enough offering to be enjoyed on its own or accompanying roast pheasant or duck.

The Brewhouse

ADDRESS Cnr Te Aute & Havelock Roads, Havelock North **PHONE** (025) 425 299 **FAX** (06) 877 3007 **BREWER** Brendan Whinham

The Brewhouse in Havelock North services about ten retail outlets in the Hawke's Bay/Rotorua region, providing kegs of mainstream beers from which customers can fill their own 2-litre pets. Brendan Whinham is the brewer, and his goal is to brew beers that meet the customers' preference at a competitive price. Two of Brendan's brews won awards in the 1996 New Zealand Beer and Food Festival. The beer is not available from the brewery and the brewery is not open to the public.

The Brewhouse Lager 4% abv

Pale to mid-straw in colour with a lemon-lime aroma, this is a crisp, clean version of the lager style. It has an interesting taste profile with very slight hop character, a little metallic, which results in a lingering dryness and a little more hop at the finish. It is a typically light quaffing lager unlikely to offend and good for washing down the sausages off the campfire.

FACT Brewing was usually done in the home as an adjunct to baking and was the province of the women of the house. In England the early taverns were run by women brewers or 'alewives', who advertised their wares by hanging an 'alestake' — most likely to be a primitive tap or strainer — over their doors.

The Brewhouse Draught 4% abv

This tan-coloured ale style has a fruit and malt aroma and a crisp, clean texture. It is reasonably sweet with no discernible hoppiness and a slight tin-can finish. It will appeal to the mainstream brown-beer drinker looking for an alternative to offerings from the bigger breweries. Serve it with Mediterranean dishes like lamb kebabs.

The Brewhouse Dark 4% abv

Very dark brown, almost black in colour, this version of a dark beer has a malt and chocolate aroma. Quite sweet with a smooth, easy-to-drink texture, it has the chocolate/coffee flavour commonplace in this style. Some complexity is evident, with a slight butterscotch aftertaste. It has a better mouth-feel and more body than many. Try it with roasted game meats.

Shamrock Brewing Company

ADDRESS 267 Main Street, Palmerston North **PHONE** (06) 355 2130
FAX (06) 358 3782 **BREWER** Daniel Hosking **OPEN** 10 am–late Mon–Sat, 10 am–6 pm Sun

Thrown in the deep end after one week's training as a brewer, former panelbeater Daniel Hosking had to teach himself to swim. Daniel is brewing to the recipe of the Shamrock brewers that came before him, providing well-established beer styles for the brew-pub's patrons. The attractive, compact brewery is visible in the dining area of the pub, where patrons can have a meal and watch Daniel in action. The beer is available on site over the bar and in kegs and flagons. Brewing takes place on Thursdays.

Shamrock Strong Bitter 4% abv

This offering, the colour of deep molasses and with a chocolate/caramel aroma, tastes just like roasted coffee beans. It even has the same bitterness on the middle palate. As with many beers, the flavour profile varies greatly depending on the temperature of the beer. At a slightly warmer temperature, Shamrock Strong Bitter has a little sweetness and therefore balance. The texture is crisp and clean and the flavour lasts down the back palate. This beer is best enjoyed at room temperature and with hot roast beef and Yorkshire pudding.

Shamrock Dark 4% abv

Very dark brown, just short of black in colour, this beer has a most interesting aroma best compared with the cowshed at milking time — warm and rich. The flavour is not so heady, more warm toast in character with mild maltiness and milder hop. It has less finish than the bitter and is probably a little lighter still. Another popular beer with the locals, it will go well with a curry.

Shamrock Draught 4% abv

A rich brown-gold colour makes this a pretty beer in the glass. There is no discernible aroma and the texture is very light. Malt and biscuit-like flavours dominate, making it an easy-to-drink quaffer popular with Shamrock patrons. Enjoy with a pie for lunch.

Shamrock Stout 4% abv

This is a very dark, almost black beer with a coffee and molasses aroma similar to the bouquet you get when removing the lid from a golden syrup tin. The texture is smooth and clean but there is no great length. The flavour exhibits coffee and malt-sweetness influences on the front and sides of the palate, with little sign of residual hop bitterness. A pleasant enough beer in the dark ale style, it will go well with a generous serving of battered oysters.

Shamrock Lager 4% abv

A somewhat darker than expected lager, this beer is straw-gold in colour. It has no aroma to speak of, and a clean rather than crisp finish. The flavour is dominated by a malt sweetness and some fruitiness, with little evidence of hop character to provide that much needed length. It is a beer style that has many fans and fits easily into the mainstream lager category. This is a palate freshener to take next time you are invited to a Mexican meal.

Tui Brewery (DB Breweries)

ADDRESS Main Road, Mangatainoka, Pahiatua **PHONE** (06) 376 7549 **FAX** (06) 376 9799 **BREWER** Colin Greig **TOURS** Mon–Fri, by arrangement

Tui Brewery was established at Mangatainoka in the lower North Island in 1889 by an entrepreneur named Henry Wagstaff. After having a succession of owners, Tui was taken over by DB Breweries in 1969. A massive modernisation programme was undertaken in the following decades and today Tui Brewery is a significant employer in the local community and supports many local events in the region. More than 100 years on, Tui East India Pale Ale is as popular as it was when Henry Wagstaff brewed the beer by hand and delivered it around the district by horse and cart. Tui is now selling from Wellington in the south to Taupo and Whakatane in the north, although you can find it in selected retail outlets nation-wide.

Tui East India Pale Ale 4% abv

Tui is a medium brown colour and has a malty, chocolate aroma with a hint of caramel as well. The texture is full bodied, smooth and mouth-filling, with a short finish. This flavourful beer has a strong malty influence with plenty of residual sweetness and some mild chocolate influence as well. There is little overt hop character but there is some dryness when the beer is enjoyed at room temperature. Tui is a refreshing mainstream match for hearty red meats — beef and lamb, roasts, grills and stews. It will also be an excellent accompaniment for pizza shared with friends.

Burridges Brewery

ADDRESS Queen Street North, Masterton **PHONE & FAX** (06) 377 1102 **BREWER** Adrian Harrison **OPEN** from 11 am daily **TOURS** by arrangement

Burridges Brewery is located at the Horseshoe Tavern in the heart of the central North Island town of Masterton. Installed in 1990, Burridges is the domain of April Lynn and her husband, who are determined to provide their patrons with high-quality, craft-brewed beer as an alternative to the mainstream beer that they also serve in the tavern. The Masterton district has had a brewery since 1877 and this new one takes the name of the Burridge family, the last private owner of the brewery before it was sold to New Zealand Breweries and subsequently closed down in 1954. While today's recipes are different, the beers produced by Burridges retain the original names. The fully operational brewery is in clear view of patrons, and a licensed restaurant is also part of the complex.

Burridges Lansdowne Lager 4.5% abv

This beer is honey-gold in colour with a slightly yeasty aroma that also gives off hints of tropical fruit and marmalade. The body is very light with negligible mouth-feel, but it goes down smoothly enough. Dominant flavours are of citrus and some slight malt with no real hop to speak of. The overall effect is of a somewhat bitter beer that will serve as a quaffer for those seeking a thirst quencher. It's not a great food beer, so save it for the beach.

Burridges Brown Jug 4% abv

Dark brown in colour — as you would expect with a name like Brown Jug — this beer also has an amber tint to it. The aroma is of chocolate, coffee and molasses, and the texture is crisp, clean and fresh. Familiar flavours of chocolate and caramel come through, along with a fair degree of malt sweetness and a touch of hop bitterness at the back of the palate. Serve this with salami and pickles on rye for a flavourful combination.

Wairarapa Brewer's Draught 4% abv

This beer, made using a top-fermenting yeast, is orange-gold in colour and has a honey, almost dessert-wine aroma to it. On the palate it is only very slightly carbonated, which highlights its thinness. The flavour evokes cut hay and there are some leathery notes there too. It has a very short length ending in a slight bitterness, almost sourness.

To prevent this quality from dominating I would recommend a strongly flavoured food, perhaps with some form of citrus influence.

Parrot & Jigger

ADDRESS Station Village, 499 Hutt Road, Lower Hutt **PHONE** (04) 566 0712 **FAX** (04) 566 0713 **BREWER** Glen Collier **OPEN** 9 am–late daily

The Parrot & Jigger is a smart little brew-pub backing onto the railway platform at the Station Village in Lower Hutt. The pub, which incorporates a fully licensed restaurant, is open seven days a week and attracts a great group of loyal regulars as well as 'tourists' from all over the region seeking out the beer for which the Parrot & Jigger has become famous. For five years Glen Collier has been the brewmaster. He believes in producing good-quality, interesting beers and includes in his range some for the less adventurous drinker and others for those who like a bigger, more challenging style. Every six weeks or so, as a special treat for his customers, Glen brews a special beer, keeping variety and experimentation alive. His beers are available on tap and in pets to take away. If ginger beer is to your liking try Glen Collier's alcoholic ginger beer.

Valley Pale 4% abv

Pale straw in colour with a sweet hop and honey aroma, Valley Pale is a good example of the lager style. It is crisp and clean with a certain freshness that adds to its appeal. A popular beer with customers, this is well balanced, medium-sweet with a hop bitterness on the middle palate. It finishes with a flourish, making it a good beer to take to that Indian or Thai restaurant.

Piston Draught 4% abv

Light gold in colour with an appealing, thick, creamy head, this beer is only slightly aromatic with a little bit of tropical fruit evident. It fits into the mainstream New Zealand draught category, easy-drinking with a grassy flavour and low hop bitterness. It also has an interesting characteristic that reminds me of freshly baked biscuits! It's best drunk very fresh and enjoyed with a hearty ploughman's lunch.

Stoker Dark 4% abv

This red-amber beer is made using a top-fermenting yeast. On the nose you pick up aromas of cherries and blackberries and some more of that biscuity character. The cherry character appears again as a flavour, along with a hint of dark chocolate. It has good levels of malt and a nice bitterness towards the end. It is smooth and clean in texture and I think a good match with bangers and mash accompanied with a dash of HP Sauce!

Nor'wester Strong Pale Ale 6% abv

This yellow-gold pale ale has sweet honey and tropical fruit aromas. The texture is crisp and clean with plenty of body. But it is the flavour balance that I really found appealing: it's lush and complex with lovely grass and herb flavours and enough honey and fruit input to complete the mix. For those of us who like our hops there is enough to satisfy. This award-winning beer makes a good partner to spicy food as well as a tasty tomato-based pasta with plenty of additional herbs like basil, thyme and sage.

Sou'wester Strong Dark Stout 6% abv

Another beer that really appealed to my palate, this one is very dark with a creamy head and heaps of malt and caramel on the nose. Made using an ale yeast and remaining unfiltered, this smooth offering has lovely, rich, chocolate and coffee flavours with no hint of the bite or sourness associated with other beers in this style. It has a long conditioning time and is a very easy-drinking dark beer that cries out for oysters *au naturel*!

Polar Brewery

ADDRESS 47 Udy Street, Petone, Lower Hutt **PHONE** (025) 419 144 **E-MAIL** polar@brewing.co.nz **BREWER** Carl Vasta

Carl Vasta's story is an interesting one and if you manage to catch him on your travels you might get him to share it with you. In 1995 Carl and two shareholders started Polar Brewery on the site of the Petone Workingmen's Club with the intention of supplying the club with a selection of mainstream beers. That venture has been successful and the distribution of the beers has expanded to include other clubs, as well as the Big Chill Café in nearby Lower Hutt and the Bodega Bar & Café in Wellington Central. Now Carl has expanded the range and is making a selection of classic beers in the boutique style. These are soon to be packaged and made more widely available. In the meantime, if you want to try Polar Brewery products you will have to visit the club or another outlet in Lower Hutt where they are sold.

Polar India Pale Ale 4% abv

Copper-gold with an orange tinge, this beer has a reasonably intense hop aroma that indicates the generous use of hops — as you would expect in an IPA. The texture is crisp and clean with plenty of mouth-feel. The flavour is full and somewhat nutty, with a mild melon character and some residual sweetness from the malt. The hop flavour is medium strength and comes through with the appropriate level of bitterness on the back palate. A good rendition of the style, it makes a fine partner for food of the spicy kind. Go with king prawns in a masala curry sauce.

Polar Draught 4% abv

The colour of golden syrup, this version of a Kiwi brown beer has a malty aroma with a touch of honey showing itself as well. Crisp and clean best describes the texture, while the flavour is a good balance of sweetness and mild hop character. There is good mouth-feel and a reasonably short finish, the malt maintaining its influence until the last. It is a good quaffing style sure to be popular with the average beer drinker and with those looking for a match with their grilled lamb chops.

Polar Dark 4% abv

A fascinating shade of red and chocolate brown, this beer presents with a thick, creamy white head. The texture, however, is much finer than you might expect. It has good mouth-feel that stays right through the middle palate. There is a high level of malt sweetness in the flavour with the same molasses/coffee flavours common in many New Zealand black beers but without the over-zealous burnt-coffee bitterness. This interpretation has a short finish and will appeal to those on their first exploration of the style. Another good food beer from Polar, this one is ideal with beef Wellington.

Polar Lager 4% abv

Golden brown in colour, this beer has a gentle aroma of malt and hops, cut grass, honey and new leather. The texture is light and crisp with a luscious mouth-feel as the beer warms. This is a full-flavoured beer with lots of rich malt character balanced by some mild hop influences. There are also some herb flavours that make the whole effect very interesting. A tasty, pleasant-drinking beer with good length, it has a finish in which you may find some mild citrus influence from the hops. Any number of moderately flavoured dishes would partner this beer well, but just for the heck of it I'd serve it with fish in a beer batter with wedges of lemon.

Polar White Beer 4% abv

Ever so slightly cloudy, this beer is a pale golden colour. It has a rich tropical-fruit, slightly peppery and obvious wheat aroma. It has medium body and a moderately creamy texture with fuller mouth-feel. The flavour profile is somewhat yeasty with some malt and clove influences. There is only a very, very mild hop character with a low-to-medium bitterness. On the back it is slightly acidic with a full finish. The alert may pick up some mild fruit esters at this point. An excellent example of its style, it is a beer well worth seeking out. When I tasted it my palate craved bread stuffed with sausage in the European tradition, but a home-made bacon and egg pie would do the trick.

The Loaded Hog Brewery

ADDRESS 14–18 Bond Street, Wellington **PHONE** (04) 472 9160
FAX (04) 472 9563 **BREWER** Rob Harrow **OPEN** 11 am–late daily

The Wellington Loaded Hog Brewery is part of a nation-wide chain of restaurant/bars. The beer brewed in Wellington is also served at the Loaded Hog at Palmerston North. For full details and tasting notes, see pages 30–32.

South Island breweries

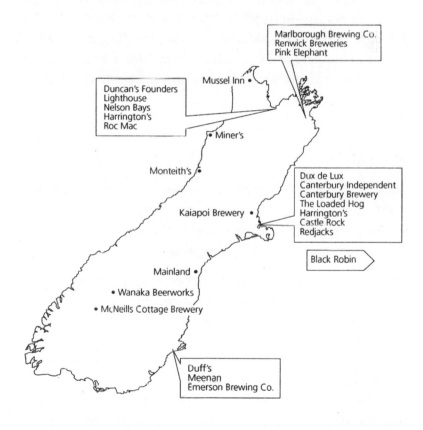

Marlborough Brewing Co.
Renwick Breweries
Pink Elephant

Duncan's Founders
Lighthouse
Nelson Bays
Harrington's
Roc Mac

Mussel Inn •

• Miner's

Monteith's •

Dux de Lux
Canterbury Independent
Canterbury Brewery
The Loaded Hog
Harrington's
Castle Rock
Redjacks

Kaiapoi Brewery •

Black Robin

Mainland •

• Wanaka Beerworks

• McNeills Cottage Brewery

Duff's
Meenan
Emerson Brewing Co.

Black Robin Brewery

ADDRESS PO Box 15, Kaingaroa, Chatham Islands **PHONE** (03) 305 0234
BREWER Leigh Thompson **TOURS** by arrangement

Undoubtedly New Zealand's most remote beer producer, Black Robin Brewery began life as a malt-extract brewery in about 1994. However, since July 1996 it has been a 1200-litre capacity full malt brewery under the watchful eye of consultant Nathan McCrorie, resident brewer at Renwick Brewery in Blenheim. Three beers are brewed on the island: Island Gold, Island Draught and Black Gold. All are 4% abv. They are available from the brewery and in stubbies from selected outlets on the mainland. Unfortunately no beer was available for tasting in time for publication.

Mussel Inn

ADDRESS Onekaka (halfway between Takaka and Collingwood) **PHONE & FAX** (03) 525 9241 **E-MAIL** musselinn@xtra.co.nz **BREWER** Andrew Dixon **OPEN** 11 am–late daily from Labour weekend to Easter, evenings only Thu–Sat during winter

The Mussel Inn Bush Café is a wonderful discovery halfway between Takaka and Collingwood, in the north of the South Island. Owned by Andrew Dixon, the Inn is an unpretentious and friendly place where locals and tourists stop to enjoy good beer and food. The Inn, to the delight of Andrew and his regulars, really defies categorisation. One minute it can be a friendly coffee shop while a couple of hours later it's a rip-roaring party. Andrew, a home-brewer from way back, built the brewery in 1995 to indulge his passion and to provide good

FACT It was accepted practice in Babylon 4000 years ago that, for a month after the wedding, the bride's father would supply his son-in-law with all the mead he could drink. Mead is a honey beer, and because the Babylonian calendar was lunar based, this period was called the 'honey moon'.

beer for his customers. Today the busy little enterprise brews all its own beers using pure water from the native forests of Kahurangi National Park At maximum production the brewery produces two brews of 300 hectolitres per week, making it one of the smallest craft breweries in New Zealand. When visiting the Inn, be sure to inquire about special brews. Each year, around late March, Andrew and his team make a couple of brews using the hops growing around the front of the Mussel Inn — an unknown variety producing quite a different flavour. No formal tours are available but if you're interested in having a look around, ask at the bar for Andrew and if he's available he'll be happy to do the honours. In addition to the beers listed below, Andrew makes a Pale Whale Ale 6% abv and a Bitter Ass 4% abv which were not available for tasting.

Golden Goose Lager 4% abv

This beer is bright yellow-gold and has a hoppy aroma with some malt sweetness. The texture is crisp and clean with good mouth-feel and a pleasant freshness. On the palate the flavours tend towards the sweet end of the spectrum, although there is a slight bitterness on the back. Not having a great deal of length, this is a moderately lightweight beer, with the hop treatment raising its game. It would be good with spicy food — how about home-made chilli meatballs?

Dark Horse Stout 4% abv

Chocolate-brown tending towards dark amber in colour, this beer has an aroma that is full-on coffee beans and fruitcake. It has a good mouth-feel, and the texture is moderately creamy and fresh. The flavour mix is complex, with fruit, chocolate and hazelnut competing for dominance and a strong hop bitterness on the back leaving its mark on the finish. It has plenty of length and may be a touch dry for some. This is a big, robust beer that cries out for similarly robust food — roast beef or lamb shanks is my call.

Captain Cooker Manuka Beer 4% abv

You will either love or hate this brave beer. Slightly cloudy red-gold in colour, it is highly aromatic, with distinct floral and sarsaparilla (root beer) characters. It has a creamy texture with lots of length and the flavour is exactly what is promised by the aroma — floral and sarsaparilla-ish with a hint of citrus. It is a highly complex beer, full of flavour and promise. It's hard to determine a perfect match but, with its flavour and aroma variety, I would enjoy it with antipasto.

Strong Ox 6% abv

In the glass Strong Ox is very dark brown with a red tinge. Malt sweetness, caramel and chocolate make up the aroma, while the texture is wonderfully smooth and creamy. The mouth-feel is this beer's great strength, but the flavour too is strong, with a good level of sweetness and bitterness balanced by some chocolate and fruit. This is a good supping beer to enjoy with your next roast of game meat — say wild venison.

White Heron Wheat Beer 5% abv

Cloudy pale straw is the best way to describe the colour of this offering. The aroma is citrusy and yeasty with hints of grapefruit and Juicyfruit chewing gum. The texture is lush and slightly grainy, while the flavour is mildly fruity and floral with a touch of the citrus characteristics. It is a very subtle beer with the usual wheat-beer characteristics understated. A short length is another feature, this one providing a freshness. It would be ideal with fish — grilled hapuku steak with a lemon beurre blanc.

Duncan's Founders Brewery

ADDRESS Founders Historic Park, 87 Atawhai Drive, Nelson **PHONE** (03) 548 4638 **FAX** (03) 548 4518 **E-MAIL** DBS@ls.co.nz **BREWER** John Duncan

This 1200-litre brewery became operational early in 1999. Brewer John Duncan is brewing and bottling a range of organic beers, cider and other organic beverages. A café, The Brewer's Daughter, and museum of Nelson brewing memorabilia is part of the complex. No beer was available at the time of writing.

Lighthouse Brewery

ADDRESS 280 Hardy Street, Nelson **PHONE** (03) 548 8983 **E-MAIL** lighthousebrewery@xtra.co.nz **BREWER** Dick Tout **OPEN** 9.30 am– 5.15 pm Mon–Fri, 9.30 am–12.30 am Sat

Lighthouse Brewery, named after New Zealand's second oldest lighthouse, at the entrance to Nelson harbour, has been open since 1996. Friendly owner Dick Tout is a beer fanatic extraordinaire. A keen home-brewer and retailer of home-brew products, Dick decided there were ways to take his passion to the masses and so opened the brewery in a shop in the heart of Nelson. Tiny in comparison with many other craft breweries, Lighthouse brews in batches of 200 litres, making it perhaps the smallest legal brewery in the country. The beers are brewed to Dick's own taste as well as that of his loyal customer base. The beers are available from the brewery in riggers and from some local restaurants.

Lighthouse Lager 4.5% abv

A vibrant mid-gold in colour with a light hop and honey aroma, Lighthouse Lager has a crisp and clean texture both at room temperature and ice cold. The flavour is mild, with a little malt and some hop and citrus character. The beer has good length, especially as it warms, and an overall freshness about it. It will be good with mussels in sautéed garlic and lemon.

Lighthouse Dark Ale 4.5% abv

The Dark Ale is a very dark chocolate-brown colour and has a light molasses and Christmas-fruit aroma. The texture is smooth and fine without being creamy, giving it a crisp rather than lush mouth-feel. Chocolate characters come to mind as flavour; it's almost smoky and slightly medicinal on the back palate. Some bitterness lingers as an aftertaste, making this an interesting offering all round. It will be good with food cooked over an open flame — grilled steak or even smoked fish.

Lighthouse Classic Stout 5% abv

Another deep brown beer with an eye-catching, thick, creamy head, this one has an aroma that is perfumed and smoky at the same time — and as it warms you get the whiff of banana. In fact the complex and ever-changing aroma is a good talking point. It is smooth and creamy and sticks to the back palate for a long finish. The flavour is of malt and sweet dark chocolate with a hint of cold coffee. A hearty winter reviver, try it as a tipple to accompany smoked sausage and a garlic kumara mash.

Nelson Bays Brewery

ADDRESS 89 Pascoe Street, Tahunanui, Nelson **PHONE & FAX** (03) 547 8097 **E-MAIL** baysbrew@ts.co.nz **BREWER** Brett Newcombe **OPEN** 11 am–5 pm Mon–Thu, 11 am–6 pm Fri & Sat

Nelson Bays Brewery, commonly known as Bays Brewery, has been operating since December 1993. The company is owned by a diverse range of shareholders, including hoteliers, beer enthusiasts, engineers and builders. The brewery produces draught beers, primarily as a cost-effective alternative to the products of the bigger breweries. Its main focus is the Nelson Bays area, but product is also available in Blenheim and Wellington, where the beer is marketed as Capital Brown, as well as in riggers at the brewery door.

Bays Gold Lager 4.2% abv
Pale straw in colour and with a light hop and malt aroma, this lager is another example of the lager style Kiwis have come to love. It has a crisp and clean texture with no great mouth-feel and little length. The flavour tends to the sweet side of the ledger and there are some lime and orange notes as well. It's a good summer quaffer to have with a barbecue, perhaps chicken satay.

Bays Draught Ale 4% abv
This is a standard Kiwi brown beer, golden syrup in colour with a thick, creamy head when poured. It has a very mild aroma, quite

sweet with a touch of honey. The texture is clean and crisp, and the flavour mild, with some malt and hop showing through. The finish is sweet and short. A good version of a popular mainstream style, it is an after-match quaffer to go with hot savouries.

Bays Dark Ale 4% abv

A deep amber hue and a thick, creamy head provide the first impressions of this beer, which uses roasted barley rather than roasted malt. The aroma is of molasses and coffee. The texture is lightweight, making it easy to drink, and it has lots of Christmas-cake flavours, especially at the front of the palate. A popular winter warmer, it's also one to have as you feast on those wonderful Nelson oysters!

Harleys Premium Ale 4% abv

This beer has quite a history to it, which will undoubtedly be shared with you by loyal locals who remember its origins fondly. It is mid-gold in colour and is reasonably aromatic, quite perfumey. In the mouth it is crisp and clean with little overt bodyweight. It has a floral, slightly wheaty flavour and a reasonably dry finish. It is a serious alternative for those who like light hop influence and are seeking maximum economy. A Thai curry will bring out those floral notes.

Harrington's Brewery

ADDRESS 53 Beach Road, Nelson **PHONE & FAX** (03) 544 8675
BREWER Craig Harrington **OPEN** 10 am–6 pm Mon–Wed, 10 am–7 pm Thu–Sat

Harrington's Brewery in Nelson is an off-shoot of its parent in Christchurch. Craig, the brewer in Nelson, is the son of John who owns Harrington's in Christchurch. Craig opened the

Nelson operation in 1997 with a view to sharing Harrington's beers with patrons in the upper South Island. Some of the beers available in Christchurch — the Draught, Big John and Traditional Dark (see page 114) — are also available in Nelson. At the same time Craig, who is passionate about his hops, brews additional beers one of which — the Best Bitter — is also available at Harrington's in Christchurch. At the moment the Nelson range is available only in flagons directly from the brewery or on tap from the Builder's Arms in Blenheim. Craig is working towards supplying packaged product.

Harrington's Best Bitter 5% abv

The dark copper colour of this offering looks good in the glass, while the distinct aroma of peaches and pears with clear evidence of hops is immediately appealing. In the mouth it is rich and mouth-filling, has plenty of body and is full of flavour. The taste is of malt and caramel with a good level of hop bitterness and some welcome dryness on the back palate. Choose full-flavoured meat dishes to go with this beer — black-pepper steak comes to mind.

Harrington's Finest Lager 5% abv

Pale to mid-straw in colour, this beer has a fairly strong aroma heavy with cut grass and tropical fruit influences. The texture is clean with

FACT In ancient times most everyday or table beer was of the small beer category, moderate in alcohol and light in body. Stronger ales were served in taverns and at village celebrations and special brews were often made for weddings, christenings, funerals and seasonal festivities.

a little stickiness, and on the back palate it is slightly dry. It is light on flavour in the New Zealand light-lager style and has only moderate hop bitterness, which many will find appealing. Easy-drinking, it will pair well with hot and spicy food such as salami on rye.

Harrington's Wheat Beer 5% abv

Pale yellow-gold with a light, distinctively white head and a low level of carbonation, this beer has an aroma of milled grain and a medium malt-fruit sweetness. It is well balanced in texture, with good mouth-feel and a light hop bitterness. The flavour is mild and slightly dusty, with evidence of fruit and the wheat. This is a beer with a certain appeal, well made and likely to partner herbaceous and sweeter food well. Just for interest I would serve it with sweet and sour fish or something similar.

Harrington's Stout 5% abv

As you would expect, this one is very dark brown in colour, with a slight amber hue. The aroma is full, with lots of chocolate and toffee character and a touch of caramel. As it warms there is also a smoky, burnt-coffee influence. The mouth-feel is smooth and a little creamy with plenty of length. Sweeter coffee and Christmas-fruit flavours dominate the palate, giving it porter-like characteristics. A mainstream example of the style, lightweight with good length, it will go well with a hot smoked-beef sandwich.

Harrington's Tasman Lager 6.5% abv

A full-strength lager with a hell of a kick, this beer is a real yellow-gold in colour. The aroma is quite subtle, with a bit of hop making its mark. The texture is clean and crisp, the mouth-feel full and satisfying. On the palate it has plenty of bite, some sweetness and lots of hop influence. There is ample length, with moderate hop bitterness and a pleasant dry character. A flavourful lager, it will go best with equally loud food. Just for fun try it with your favourite hamburger from the local takeaway!

Roc Mac

ADDRESS 660 Main Road, Stoke, Nelson **PHONE** (03) 547 5357 **FAX** (03) 547 6876 **BREWER** Tracy Banner **TOURS** 11.15 am daily during autumn/winter, with an extra 2 pm tour during summer

The Mac's range of all-malt ales and lagers is batch-brewed at Roc Mac, formerly the McCashin's Brewery & Malthouse, in Stoke, Nelson. McCashin's was considered by some to be the first commercial microbrewery to offer any serious competition to the two big brewers, Lion and DB. However, from the outset the brewery produced a different style of beer. Its brewing philosophy determined that Mac's beer products adhere to the Reinheitsgebot, the Bavarian beer purity law of 1516, which countenances no use of chemicals, preservatives, artificial colourings or other adjuncts. Without doubt this positioning attracted many customers earlier in the company's development. Over recent years the appeal has broadened and now Mac's has a solid following throughout the country.

Mac's Gold 4% abv

Perhaps the most famous of all the Mac's products, the Gold is in fact light straw in colour and carries a substantial, creamy head. Fruit and hops are present in the aroma, with suggestions of citrus and honey as well. The texture is light and clean with moderate mouth-feel. Subtle is the best way to describe the flavour: the malt comes through and there is some mild bitterness towards the end, as well as a suggestion of yeastiness. The finish, while short, is refreshing. For a food match I suggest roast chicken with a well-herbed stuffing.

Mac's Ale 4% abv

In the glass this beer is mid-brown with a red tinge. The head is white and thick. Wafts of fruit with some cut-hay influence form the aroma, while the texture is smooth and moderately creamy. Mac's Ale is a reasonably mainstream beer with broad appeal, having strong malt influences balanced with some hop character. You may detect a slight citrus taste as well. It's a good quaffing beer to enjoy with your main course — I'd choose roast beef from the menu.

Mac's Premium Reserve 5.2% abv

Mid-straw in colour, this beer has a creamy white head but a very mild aroma with only the most subtle malt notes showing through. The texture is rich and creamy with plenty of mouth-feel, while the flavour is sweet and malty with strong caramel and some yeasty influences as well. There is low-level hop bitterness but it comes through only at the end. An interesting beer that will appeal to those looking for something to sup and savour, it would be worth trying with creamy chicken fettuccine.

Mac's Special Light 1% abv

It's not easy to make a light beer that has full flavour and the characters of a regular-strength beer. Mac's Special Light, however, is a reasonably good example. Pale straw in colour with a moderately bitter aroma of grain and grass, it has a texture that is mildly creamy and a mouth-feel that is quite lightweight. The flavour is fairly hoppy, although there is a moderate level of sweetness as well. This beer has an early finish but is pleasant and refreshing enough. Many foods will dominate, so choose subtlety. I'd go for white fish poached in white wine and seasoned with freshly ground pepper.

Black Mac 4% abv

A deliciously dark brown colour marks Black Mac, which ranks as one of the first 'dark' beers — at least in modern times — to strike the palate of the Kiwi beer drinker. Its aroma is of Christmas cake and malt, while the texture is rich and smooth and moderately creamy, making it a good beer to drink through the head. Gentle flavours of malt and caramel dominate and I also detected some pleasant nuttiness. There is good length and a malt sweetness to the finish. Enjoy this with Nelson oysters.

Mac's Extra 7% abv

On the label this beer is referred to as a strong malt lager. It is mid-straw in colour and has a strong aroma of malt, molasses and some wheat. As it warms it becomes perfumey and slightly floral. In texture the Extra is creamy with a suggestion of graininess. The flavour is full and sweet with some honey and citrus influence and a slightly dry, slightly bitter finish. I liked the balance of this beer and its comparatively complex make-up. I suggest it is a good food beer, one that will work well in partnership with roast pork.

Marlborough Brewing Company

ADDRESS Grove Road, Blenheim   **PHONE & FAX** (03) 577 8348
BREWER Rob Stephens

The Marlborough Brewing Company was set up in 1992 by a group of publicans and liquor retailers looking to provide their customers with high-quality beers at a reasonable price. Today the brewery remains a production facility serving the requirements of its shareholders in the Marlborough area. It produces three mainstream beers and a 'steam beer', all distinguished by their bright and cheerful packaging. They can be purchased from most liquor stores and many pubs, bars and restaurants in Blenheim and the surrounding districts.

Marlborough Gold 4% abv

This very mild beer is yellow-gold in colour and has a light malt and hop aroma with a bit of mealy character for good measure. The body is smooth and crisp, the flavour mildly hoppy and quite sweet without much lingering fullness. It's a very light, easy-to-drink quaffer in the lager style, appealing to those who prefer sweetness to dryness. It's another to enjoy with spicy food.

Red Devil 3.9% abv

A dark golden colour characterises the appearance of Red Devil, with a mildly malty and slightly yeasty aroma adding to first impressions. The texture is crisp and clean with no real aftertaste of note. The flavour is very very mild, somewhat sweet with the merest trace of hop. There is nothing complex about this beer, so be sure to choose a food match that is equally subtle and will not overpower the beverage — say white fish pan-fried in a little butter and lightly seasoned with ground pepper.

Marlborough Draught 4% abv

An interesting tan-brown, with perhaps a slight red tinge, the Draught has the strongest aroma of the beers in the Marlborough range. It's malty and smoky with a bit of caramel and a lingering cut-grass character about it. On the palate it is mildly creamy with good mouth-feel and a welcome degree of residual flavour. The smoky, almost peaty, qualities come through in the flavour as well, and are joined by a hint of peanut. This is a good food beer with plenty of interesting components. I would serve it with roasted wild duck or pheasant — just for a treat.

Original Steam Beer 5% abv

The colour of golden syrup, this beer has a mildly yeasty aroma with some evidence of malt sweetness. The texture is smooth and clean with no real mouth-feel. The flavour, which is yeasty with some hop bitterness evident on the middle palate, disappears quickly, making it quite refreshing. It is suitable to accompany most fish dishes except the more highly flavoured, which may tend to overwhelm this very mild beer.

Renwick Breweries

ADDRESS Inkerman Street, Renwick, Blenheim **PHONE** (03) 572 9328 **FAX** (03) 572 9325 **BREWER** Nathan McCrorie **OPEN** noon–10 pm Sun–Tue, 11 am–11 pm Wed–Sat **TOURS** by arrangement

Englishman Bill Penfold and his wife Marilyn in 1991 established Renwick Breweries as the first craft brewery in Marlborough. A few years and some difficult times later they built the Cork & Keg English-style pub on the same site — and have never looked back. The brewery supplies English-style beer to the pub, which entices regulars, passers-by and special-event groups with ploughman's lunches, pork pies and a variety of traditional 'pub grub'. The beer is available on site and brewery tours can be easily arranged. Try some of Bill's cider while you're there — it's pretty damn good.

Hurricane Premium 5% abv

This is Renwick's trademark beer, the one the regular patrons love. It has a golden-syrup colour and a molasses and fruit aroma. In the mouth it is creamy and smooth with a good mouth-filling quality and a rich body. The flavour is medium-sweet with malt and fruit evident and, in keeping with local preferences, only a mild residual hop bitterness. The higher alcohol content assists in carrying the flavour around the palate. I would try it with a serving of full and flavourful spaghetti bolognese.

Renwick Original Dark 4% abv

One of the first 'dark' beers in New Zealand, this version is amber-red in colour and has a fruity, sweet-malt aroma. The texture is creamy with no great back-palate influence. The flavour too is sweet, with light, mild malt and hop characters. This is another good version of a session beer, nothing too complex and brewed with mass appeal in mind. Take it to a barbecue or serve it with steak and kidney pie.

Renwick Natural Draught 4% abv

This bottom-fermented beer is copper-gold in the lager style, with a sweet fruit and malt aroma and a fresh, clean texture. There is some evidence of malt fruitiness in the flavour but the sweetness of the aroma does not transfer to the palate. Rather there is some lingering hop bitterness, which gives this beer a lift. I suggest serving this good quaffing draught with a hearty portion of roast beef.

Renwick Pilsner Lager 4% abv

The label describes this as pure malt lager, and that is a reasonably accurate description of the style. It is very pale straw in colour and has a crisp and clean mouth-feel. The flavour is not complex — sweet with medium-strength hop bitterness. The length is moderate and the aftertaste very mild. Bill says this is a favourite with European travellers, who often enjoy it with a ploughman's lunch.

Southman's Draught 3.8% abv

This golden brown mainstream beer has a very mild, light malt aroma with some slight peanutty characters and a sweetness derived from the added sugar. The texture is light and clean, and the flavour mild, sweet and without any great challenge to the palate. There is no pretence about this offering, which is brewed to satisfy the brewery's regular brown-beer patrons who have no great love of the hop. Try it with one of the Cork & Keg's pork pies.

Pink Elephant Brewery

ADDRESS Rapaura Road, Renwick, Marlborough **PHONE & FAX** (03) 572 9467 **BREWER** Roger Pink **OPEN** 11 am–5 pm Wed–Sun **TASTINGS** by arrangement

Open since December 1990, the colourfully named Pink Elephant Brewery is owned by the equally colourful Roger Pink. Roger is an Englishman who has set out to mimic the beer styles of his homeland, and he spares no effort in reproducing exactly the right conditions. Roger produces his own special

FACT Beer was the reason the Pilgrims landed at Plymouth Rock. It's clear from the *Mayflower*'s log that the crew didn't want to waste beer looking for a better site. The log goes on to state that the passengers 'were hasted ashore and made to drink water that the seamen might have the more beer'.

malts and uses Nelson hops to produce top-fermented, naturally conditioned ales of intricate flavour and aroma for the real English-style beer aficionado. It's well worth a visit to the brewery — if you are lucky, you'll get to spend some time with the fanatical Roger Pink as a bonus. Don't bother asking what PDA or PBA means — it's his little secret! All Pink Elephant products can be purchased by mail order or direct from the brewery. Keep an eye out for Roger's special and occasional brews, among them the gold-medal-winning Roger's Reserve.

Pachyderm Stout 4% abv

A very dark chocolate brown in colour, this beer has a light aroma of coffee and molasses. It has a pleasing mouth-feel — not too light, not too creamy. The coffee characteristics come through on the palate, and there is plenty of fruit flavour balanced by some hop bitterness. The length is good with a good, dry finish. An excellent Irish-style stout, it is ideal served with roast quail in a rich gravy.

Mammoth 7% abv

The quirkily named Mammoth is a dark amber-red, aromatic with distinctive, rich, fruit and soft malt characters. The texture is rich and creamy, filling the mouth with luscious malty flavours and some dark fruit (dates and raisins), together with firm hop bitterness. These flavours linger long and strong, providing a wonderfully true ale with mammoth-sized flavour. The high alcohol content makes this an excellent aperitif and an equally good digestive if simply served with a traditional ploughman's lunch or a rich rabbit stew.

PDA 5% abv

A top-fermented ale in the style of a porter, this offering is dark brown and full of Christmas-fruit aromas derived from the generous use of dark malt. It has a freshness to it, yet at the same time it is creamy and rich. The flavour is complex, with the malt showing its head, but balanced by some residual bitterness and a hint of apple. It has good length with a pleasing dryness on the back palate. Another lovely offering from the Pink Elephant Brewery, this one could be served with a hearty roast or a traditional deep-dish steak and kidney pie.

PBA 5% abv

Another full-strength top-fermented ale, PBA is a rich golden yellow in the glass. The aroma is hoppy with some evidence of caramel and fruit coming through. In the mouth it is creamy and has the freshness that characterises all of the Pink Elephant beers. The flavour is full, with enticing residual hoppiness, some sweetness to maintain balance and a special garden-herb character as well. There is enough hop bitterness to satisfy the hop-heads and plenty of length for the rest of us. This is a lovely food beer to enjoy with a range of dishes: just for fun try it with fish and chips — without the vinegar!

Miner's Brewery

ADDRESS 10 Lyndhurst Street, Buller, West Coast **PHONE & FAX** (03) 789 6201 **E-MAIL** absalom@xtra.co.nz **BREWER** Dean Lamplough **OPEN** 8.30 am–5.30 pm Mon–Fri, 10 am–5.30 pm Sat

Originally owned by four local hoteliers, Miner's Brewery in the small West Coast town of Buller is still locally owned and operated with majority shareholders Alan and Jo Absalom firmly in charge. Support for the brewery from the 5000-strong local population is fervent; demand for Miner's brews is so strong that the beer is still delivered by the tanker-full, making

Miner's one of the few craft breweries still distributing this way. If success is measured by market share in the local area, Miner's Brewery must hold some sort of record for its influence in Buller and the West Coast region. The beers are unashamedly brewed to satisfy the tastebuds of the locals, but there is plenty of interest here for the visiting beer drinker. The range is available both from the brewery and on tap at many West Coast pubs.

Miner's Classic Gold 5% abv

This lager-style beer is pale straw in colour but in the right light could be called gold. There is a definite hop character on the nose and the texture is exactly as it should be: light and refreshing. I detected a slight graininess that added a certain character to what is certainly a mainstream product. The flavour suggests honey with the hop coming through again, and while the beer is sweet there is no lingering cloying character. In the middle there is some biscuit character, while a good level of hop bitterness is present on the back palate. This is a good session beer, especially when accompanied with whitebait fritters!

Miner's Draught 4% abv

The colour is copper-gold, and the aroma is of malty sweetness with some Christmas fruit and caramel. The texture is quite busy and the beer seems highly carbonated, making it a refreshing drink at any time of the year. On the palate the taste is malty rather than hop-oriented, although there is a little bitterness towards the back. It has a short finish and some residual sweetness. This is a good quaffer in the nature of a Kiwi brown beer, and has a bit of class that takes it above the average for this style. It will go well with most red-meat dishes — I'd serve it with venison steaks.

Miner's Dark 4% abv

A nice dark chocolate colour with a red tinge to it, this beer has an aroma that also brings to mind chocolate — with a bit of caramel/toffee thrown in for interest. The texture is crisp and clean, and the flavour has lots of depth but not much length. On the palate it tastes like cold coffee and chocolate, with malt fruitiness adding some sweetness. It has plenty of flavour on the middle palate and is akin to a porter in style, but there is little hop interest for hop-heads or body to carry the flavour through to the finish. If seeking a meal match, save it for the Sunday roast.

Monteith's Brewing Company (DB Breweries)

ADDRESS Cnr Turamaha & Herbert Streets, Greymouth **PHONE** (03) 768 4149 **FAX** (03) 768 6604 **BREWER** Keith Armstrong **TOURS** by arrangement

Monteith's Brewing Company has been a proud West Coast brewer since 1858, and has been producing Monteith's Original Ale since the coast was in the grip of gold fever. Today that illustrious tradition continues with a range of beers that are batch-brewed using coal-fired boilers, open-fermenters, natural ingredients and fresh water from the region. To complement Monteith's Original Ale, the company has introduced Monteith's Celtic Red, Monteith's Golden Lager and Monteith's Black. Brewer Keith Armstrong has gone further and recently introduced Monteith's Pilsner to the mix as well as two seasonal beers, Bock Winter Bier and Summer Ale. The range, now available throughout the country in attractive 350-millilitre bottles, is garnering a lot of interest, especially among dedicated beer lovers. Food fanciers too are finding Monteith's beers to their liking, much to the delight of Keith Armstrong, who has a firm commitment to encouraging and developing beer and food pairing.

Monteith's Original Ale 4% abv

A deep golden brown in colour, this is a classic beer in the Kiwi brown-beer style and therefore has wide appeal. It has a full, malty aroma, a crisp, clean texture and plenty of mouth-feel. There is a moderate level of hop influence, especially towards the end. The flavour is reasonably sweet with both malt and hop flavours showing through. I detected some toffee characters as well. The beer has good length and a short and pleasant aftertaste. The brewers recommend serving this with whitebait; I'd probably offer mussels in the half shell with a tomato and basil dressing.

Monteith's Golden Lager 5% abv

The colour of the lager is a bright straw with a hint of lime, while the aroma is mild with hops clearly in the mix. The texture is lightweight, clean, crisp and refreshing. It has a full flavour, rich and malty with a nutty character well balanced by a slight yeast/grass influence. The mouth-feel and length are both generous for the style and the aftertaste demonstrates both sweetness and dryness, keeping the beer interesting. Like the brewer I would go with a salmon dish — perhaps with a moderate serving of a creamy dill mayonnaise.

Monteith's Celtic Red 4.4% abv

This is an Irish-style ale with a burnt red colour and a dry, roasted malt aroma. It is crisp in texture with a mildly creamy mouth-feel, while the flavour is full of soft malt fruitiness and a crisp dryness. There are gentle roasted notes in the aftertaste. A well-rounded, smooth brew, this is a beer for the traditionalists who will enjoy its simple, uncomplicated, generous character. Any red-meat roast will partner this beer well, but in keeping with the wild West Coast spirit I'd have it with venison or spit-roasted hogget.

Monteith's Black 5.2% abv
This excellent example of the dark beer style is finding lots of followers. It is a deep dark brown colour and has a rich aroma full of malt with some roasted malt and chocolate notes as well. The texture is equally rich, although lighter in body and less creamy than you might expect. It has great mouth-feel and the flavour is of coffee and roasted chocolate — with just enough hop dryness to provide a bitter-sweet balance to the chocolate/malt character. Keith and I agree this beer is perfect with smoked eel.

Monteith's Pilsner 5% abv
Pale gold in colour, this beer has a mild aroma of cut grass and hay with some melon influence as well. The mouth-feel is full and generous, while the texture is crisp and clean. The flavour is complex, with herbal and hop characters and some spiciness providing the interest. There is residual sweetness from the malt and a pleasant dryness giving a clean and lingering aftertaste. This is a beer that the hop-heads will appreciate, although the hop influence is subtle. When considering your food match think about crayfish for a stylish twosome.

Monteith's Bock Winter Bier 6.2% abv
Released as a seasonal offering in the latter half of the year, the Bock is tawny gold in colour and has a rich malt aroma with some cut-hay influences as well. True to style, the texture is smooth and warming, while the robust flavour shows plenty of malt and hop

balance. This is a complex beer with great mouth-feel and a generous aftertaste well carried by the higher alcohol content. This is a personal favourite — for a food match I would choose something reasonably robust but not too sweet. How about goat?

Monteith's Summer Ale 5% abv

The newest beer in the Monteith's range, Summer Ale has a very soft straw colour. It has a powerful aroma of ginger and spice with some maltiness evident too. The texture is really crisp and this beer should be enjoyed ice cold to maximise the effect of the texture. It has good mouth-feel and a full flavour of malt, ginger and spice with some tropical melon flavours. It's reasonably sweet but with a very refreshing dryness towards the end. Keith recommends a wedge of orange or lime with this delightful seasonal offering. My suggestion for a meal match is cold wild pork and salad, but I'd also serve it to lunch guests with an orange sherbet.

Kaiapoi Brewery

ADDRESS Southern Grain Spirits, 9a Peraki Street, Kaiapoi **PHONE** (03) 327 6389 **FAX** (03) 327 6233 **BREWER** Peter Howard **OPEN** 8.30 am–5.30 pm Mon–Fri

Unpretentious and laid back in its approach to brewing under the control of Peter Howard, Kaiapoi Brewery provides two beers primarily for local consumption. These are not brews for the beer fanatic: they are uncomplicated quaffers, batch-brewed and basic. Having supplied local outlets such as the Kaiapoi Workingmen's Club since 1992, Kaiapoi also sells its products at its brewery at the Southern Grain Spirits plant in Kaiapoi.

Finnegans Traditional Dark Ale 4% abv

A blend of coloured malts gives this beer a dark molasses hue and a strong malt aroma with hints of coffee and old hay. It is light in body and tastes of toasted malt and molasses with a touch of burnt coffee. It has a bitter aftertaste and would benefit from some additional sweetness. For a food match I would opt for roasted pork with an apple sauce to provide balance.

Kaiapoi Draught 4% abv

Red-copper in colour, this offering has an aroma that is strongly reminiscent of hops and citrus. While the texture is lightweight, the flavour is hoppy and slightly citrusy and with a definite bitterness, almost estery/sour. There is some evidence of malt but it is very subtle. This is a satisfactory quaffing beer most likely enjoyed by locals used to Kaiapoi's distinctive style of brew. This is another option for the grilled-food meal.

Dux de Lux

ADDRESS Arts Centre, Cnr Hereford & Montreal Streets, Christchurch City **PHONE** (03) 366 6919 **FAX** (03) 366 5341 **BREWER** Richard Fife **OPEN** 11.30 am–11 pm daily

Dux de Lux can be found at the Arts Centre in the heart of New Zealand's garden city. The Dux, as it is affectionately known, was established ten years ago and has a brewing philosophy of producing natural beers that are genuine and honest in ingredients and the way they are made. The beer is brewed to appeal to those who appreciate craft-style beer and both top- and bottom-fermenting processes are used. Brewer Richard Fife produces 4000 litres per week, catering exclusively for patrons of the Dux de Lux bar and restaurant. This range of naturally brewed, award-winning beer is not available anywhere else in New Zealand and can therefore be considered a unique Christchurch experience. You may notice a similarity between the labels of the Sou'wester and the Nor'wester and two beers of the same name brewed by the Parrot & Jigger in Lower Hutt. These beers were devised at a time when there was some joint shareholding in the two companies; they are now independent of each other and, while the names and labels are the same, the beers taste quite different.

Dux Lager 4% abv
Pale yellow-gold with a light, distinctively white head and a low level of carbonation, this lager has an aroma of honeysuckle, mild hop and medium malt fruitiness. It is well balanced in texture, with good mouth-feel and a light hop bitterness in the pilsener style. The flavour is of crisp malt and plenty of fruit. A well-made beer with broad appeal, it is likely to partner spicy food well. Just for interest I would serve it with sweet and sour pork.

Blue Duck Draught 4% abv
This beer fills the glass with a vibrant red-copper colour. There is an aroma of roasted malt with some biscuity and mealy characters as well. The texture is crisp and clean, not hearty but mouth-filling. This is an easy-drinking beer in which the malt flavours shine through and you are left with a dark chocolate aftertaste. This is a good beer to partner a decent porterhouse steak with mushroom sauce.

Hereford Bitter 4% abv
The Hereford Bitter has a dark ruby colour and an aroma of caramel, rhubarb crumble and mild roast coffee. The mouth-feel is light and

fresh with a slight graininess. Coffee and malt come through as flavours and there is a medium length. This is an inoffensive traditional Kiwi-style beer with mild hop influences and broad appeal, another to serve with grilled food — or perhaps with a rich chicken cassoulet.

Nor'wester Strong Pale Ale 6.5% abv

Top-fermented in true ale style, the Nor'wester is a rich red-tan colour — almost copper — and has a sweet malt aroma with some peat and fruit. It is creamy and mouth-filling in texture and is best appreciated at room temperature. The malt comes through again as flavour and it finishes with a slightly medicinal character that is not unattractive. A multi-dimensional beer, well made, this would be perfect with roast beef.

Sou'wester Strong Dark Stout 6.5% abv

Dark and dense with a creamy head, this beer has a strong fruit malt aroma and rich, creamy texture. Although it is not mouth-filling, tending on the thin side, there is plenty of flavour — caramel, chocolate and coffee. The malt comes through on the palate and provides moderate length. This satisfying beer will appeal to dark-beer fans. I'd match it with creamy blue cheese.

Black Shag Stout 5.5% abv

This beer is dark, almost black, with a rich, creamy head that stays and stays. The aroma is of pure malt and it intensifies as the beer warms. The texture, as you would expect, is rich and creamy with plenty of mouth-feel, the flavours big and bold with an interesting combination of chocolate, fruit and stable hay. The length is just as it should be and entices you to savour another mouthful. Choose game as a meat accompaniment; the daring might go for baklava or Russian fudge cake.

Canterbury Independent Brewery

ADDRESS 472 Tuam Street, Christchurch **PHONE & FAX**
(03) 389 7730 **BREWER** Paul Hogan

Canterbury Independent Brewery, located in central Christchurch, is a medium-sized commercial brewery offering an alternative range of products for the mainstream beer drinker. The business venture was originally owned co-operatively by ten publican shareholders who decided in 1991 they wanted some freedom of product and created Canterbury Independent to supply their own establishments. The beers are brewed in bulk and are available on tap and in riggers from about eighty outlets, including pubs and chartered clubs, from Nelson to the Bluff.

Forge Draught 4% abv

A typical New Zealand mainstream beer, this is copper-gold in colour with a sweet aroma, a fairly one-dimensional texture and a very short finish. The flavour is reasonably hoppy and slightly citrusy but without depth. It's a quaffer brewed for mass appeal and best enjoyed at a barbecue.

Hauslager Gold Label 4.6% abv

On the day I tasted it this was a slightly cloudy beer, pale straw in colour and with malt and yeast dominating the aroma, although some floral characters were evident as well. The texture is syrupy but light and the flavour bitter-sweet, akin to a wheat beer. A colleague described this beer as having some home-brew qualities. This distinctive beer is hard to categorise and probably has narrow appeal. Its yeasty character most likely lends itself to bread and cheese as a food partner.

Matson's Classic Draught 4% abv

This is another that was a little cloudy on the day I tried it. The colour is dark copper with a faint redness to it. The aroma is yeasty with a dominant biscuit character. The mouth-feel is very light, with the flavour showing some malt. Overall it's a fairly simple product, made to satisfy the easy-to-please drinker, another for the barbecue or the curry night at the neighbours'.

Matson's Strong Ale 5% abv

Copper-brown, almost gold, in colour, this offering has a very malty aroma when first poured. The texture is good with plenty of mouth-feel and body. The flavour is full, with malt fruitiness evident, giving an impression of sweetness and some complexity. While this is an ale in the mainstream category, it is easy-drinking and will partner highly flavoured food well. Game meat or a rich beer stew would be ideal.

Black Bier 4% abv

A dark reddish brown in colour, this version of a black beer has a toasted-malt aroma with some burnt-coffee characters evident as well. It is very light with little mouth-feel and a short finish. It is an easy-drinking beer and the dark chocolate and molasses flavours add some appeal. The thinness of the beer will mean it is easily

---

FACT Before thermometers were invented, some historians say, brewers would dip a thumb or finger into the mix to find the right temperature for adding yeast. Too cold, and the yeast wouldn't grow. Too hot, and the yeast would die. This thumb in the beer is where we get the phrase 'rule of thumb'.

overpowered, so when seeking a meal match try Wiener schnitzel with mushrooms.

Canterbury Brewery (New Zealand Breweries)

ADDRESS 36 St Asaph Street, Christchurch **PHONE** (03) 379 4940
FAX (03) 371 3222 **TOURS** 10.30 am Mon–Thu, and by arrangement

The imposing landmark that is Canterbury Brewery has been around in one state or another since 1854. It was formed as a result of mergers between three major Christchurch breweries — Wards, Crown and Mannings. By the time it became part of New Zealand Breweries in 1923, it had established an enduring business with the support of both the local community and the greater Canterbury region. Today Canterbury Brewery produces up to 50 million litres of beer per year on its 2.5-hectare site in the heart of Christchurch. A raft of brands comes out of the brewery but its flagship is Canterbury Draught, or CD as it is known to its friends. Tours of the brewery are well worth the visit. The Heritage Centre is fantastic and provides a great account of the history of brewing in the region and the country.

Canterbury Draught 4% abv
Originally known as Ward's Ale, Canterbury Draught is designed to satisfy today's Cantabrian while still holding true to the traditional style of its heritage. This moderately malty beer balanced with Nelson hops and rounded out with a hint of sweetness has body and flavour while remaining easy-drinking. Canterbury Draught is ideal with delicately flavoured meats such as pork, chicken and, of course, Canterbury lamb with minted potatoes.

Kilkenny 4.3% abv

New Zealand is one of eight countries world-wide allowed to brew the Irish beer Kilkenny under licence. It is distinctively ruby-red in colour, with a rich, creamy head that lasts to the very end. The texture is rich and smooth with a clean and-refreshing mouth-feel. It is an easy-drinking beer with plenty of malt and Christmas-fruit character as well as a hint of caramel and molasses. I would serve Kilkenny with game meat or with a slice of stilton before dessert.

Guinness 4.1% abv

One of the world's most popular stouts, Guinness is brewed in New Zealand under licence from its Irish parent. A deep dark chocolate-brown in colour, it is deliciously aromatic with roasted malt and coffee notes and some toffee character as well. The Guinness texture is creamy and smooth, very soft and mouth-filling. The taste is full-on roasted malt and moderate hop flavour, but with a tang of hop acidity and some spice and fruit too. It is a complex beer with a fresh dryness at the end — which is a long time coming, such is this beer's length. The classic match is oysters and it makes sense when in New Zealand to partner Guinness with some of our very fine Bluff, Nelson or Orongo Bay oysters.

The Loaded Hog Brewery

ADDRESS 39 Dundas Street, Christchurch **PHONE & FAX** (03) 377 2249 **BREWER** Rodney Burke **OPEN** 11 am–late

The Christchurch Loaded Hog Brewery is part of a nation-wide chain of restaurant/bars. The beer brewed in Christchurch is also served at the Loaded Hogs in Dunedin and Timaru. For full details and tasting notes, see pages 30–32.

Harrington's Brewery

ADDRESS 199 Ferry Road, Christchurch City **PHONE** (03) 366 6323
FAX (03) 366 3542 **E-MAIL** simonbretherton@xtra.co.nz **BREWER**
Simon Bretherton **OPEN** 10 am–8 pm Mon–Wed, 10 am–9 pm Thu,
10 am–10 pm Fri–Sat

One of the larger microbreweries in New Zealand, Harrington's
services a chain of bottle stores in Christchurch and the
Canterbury region. Catering to a general audience of
mainstream beer drinkers, Harrington's offers a wide selection
of beers in competition with the bigger brewers. Brewer Simon
Bretherton knows his stuff and aims to produce high-quality
beer that covers a range of flavour preferences while remaining
price-competitive. Harrington's beers are widely available in
both packaged and draught form from throughout the region
and from the brewery itself. Three of the beers are also
available from the Harrington's Brewery in Nelson (see page
88), owned by Craig Harrington, son of the owner of
Harrington's in Christchurch.

Harrington's Big John 6.5% abv

This ale is a light-molasses gold in colour. It has a strong aroma of
cut grass with a few citrus notes as well. It has a good texture that
fills the mouth, and is smooth but has some zest to it at the same
time. The flavour is of malt with some hop bitterness, but the
overriding impression is of a fruity, almost fortified character. The
high alcohol content is recognisable in the dryness on the sides of
the palate and some sweetness evident on the back of the throat.
This is a good beer for supping on its own, especially well chilled, or
try it at room temperature with a lamb roast complete with mint
sauce.

Harrington's Lager 4% abv

Pale gold in colour and a little cloudy, this beer has an aroma that is mildly hoppy with a touch of sugar sweetness. The texture is clean and fresh and very fine. It's not a highly flavoured beer — it will suit those who enjoy the light lager style — but it has a slight malt influence together with evidence of hops. It's a good quaffer to enjoy when you have friends over for a pizza.

Harrington's Canterbury Pale Ale 4.8% abv

The colour is very pale gold with a slight orange tint. This beer is distinguished by the use of four different malts imported from the UK. The aroma is yeasty with some malt sweetness evident as well as a hint of orange peel. The texture is rich and mouth-filling and the flavour full of malt and hazelnuts. There is plenty of length and good bitterness on the back palate. This is an interesting beer best served well chilled and enjoyed with lemon chicken.

Harrington's Finest Lager 5% abv

A thick, creamy head tops this dark gold beer. It has a slightly wheaty, slightly musty aroma to it. In the mouth it is crisp and clean with an appealing freshness. The flavour is mild with some malt fruit characters together with a good level of hop bitterness for this style. I'd match it with a spicy dish, perhaps a Malaysian beef curry.

Harrington's Kiwi Draught 4% abv

Brewed to fit into New Zealand mainstream draught style, Kiwi Draught is copper-gold and has a malty aroma with hints of caramel and old leather. It is lighter-bodied with no real length, and the flavour is sweetish rather than hoppy. This is sure to appeal to many New Zealand beer drinkers. It is an unpretentious quaffing beer best enjoyed with a few hot savouries while watching the rugby.

Harrington's Draught 4% abv

This is another copper-gold beer with similar characteristics to Kiwi Draught. There is a little more coffee and fruit in the aroma but the leather is still there. The texture is slightly more creamy but it is drier and more complex in flavour than the Kiwi. The malt flavours are more pronounced and the hops more evident. For a good partner I'd suggest a mixed grill of lamb chops, bacon and beef sausages with lashings of HP Sauce.

Harrington's Traditional Dark 4% abv

This beer is the colour of molasses — deep, deep copper with a hint of red — and has a thick, creamy, brown head. There is coffee and caramel in the aroma, but the dominant note is hokey pokey. The texture is a little lighter than expected but there is plenty of length, with flavours of roast malt and dark fruit coming through. It's slightly grabby on the back palate though interesting all the same. Try it with small pieces of a rich dark fruitcake.

Castle Rock Brewing

ADDRESS Five Star Liquor, 495 Ferry Road, Ferrymead, Christchurch
PHONE (03) 384 3121 **BREWER** Glen Wieblitz **OPEN** 9 am–6 pm Mon–Sat

Castle Rock takes its name from a local landmark, supports local rugby and has been supplying keg beer to local bars since 1988. Brewed at an average of 10,000 litres per week, the beers are now available in bars and clubs as well as Five Star Liquor stores in Christchurch and throughout the Canterbury region. The brewery caters for the mainstream Kiwi beer drinker, offering reasonably priced alternatives to major brands.

Castle Rock Extra 7% abv

Yellow-gold in colour and with a thick, creamy head, this extra-strength beer has an appealing aroma of maize, malt and the grain silo. In the mouth it is smooth and mouth-filling with good length and finish. The flavour is complex, with a good balance between the sweet and bitter. It is pleasantly dry on the throat with nothing to detract from the flavour. Although the higher alcohol content gives it a slight rawness, this is a good beer, one to have as an aperitif or with Chinese food, particularly sweet and sour chicken.

Castle Rock Wheat 4% abv

A complex recipe of hop flowers, green bullet hops and lots of extras gives this beer a straw-gold appearance and a light hop aroma with some honey characteristics when first served. The texture is light, in the pilsener style, with a short finish. The flavour is medium-sweet with a low-level hop bitterness. This is a mainstream beer in the lager style, ideal served with hot and spicy meals — perhaps a chilli con carne.

Castle Rock Gold Lager 4% abv

Yellow-gold and with a distinct aroma of peanut brittle, the Gold Lager is as you would expect — light and easy-drinking with a clean, crisp texture. The flavour is more complex, with obvious wheat and peanut characters, a touch of hop bitterness and very little sweetness. On the back palate it is dry, giving it reasonable length. Choose a food match that is creamy in texture, say fettuccine carbonara.

Castle Rock Draught 4% abv

A thick, creamy head caps this copper-gold draught from Castle Rock. There's not much on the aromatic front, the texture is light and airy, and the beer is easy-drinking. It has a very subtle flavour profile, medium-sweet with a slight hop bitterness towards the end. This is a mainstream quaffer sure to have many fans and best enjoyed with a meat meal — why not lamb chops served with roast garlic.

Castle Rock Black 4% abv

Dark brown without being black, this beer has an aroma of roasted malt and treacle and a texture that is light and refreshing. The predominant flavour is of coffee and malt, although there is a suggestion of boiled vegetables. It has a short finish, giving it an overall impression of being a highly flavoured, thin version of the style. It is not a beer to design a meal around.

Redjacks Brewing Company

ADDRESS 1060 Ferry Road, Christchurch **PHONE** (03) 384 7036 **FAX** (03) 384 3121 **BREWER** Mike Holling

This brewery began operation early in 1999 and will be producing two beers — Redjacks Draught and Redjacks Lager. No beer was available at the time of writing, but brewer Mike Holling says both should be available from selected outlets in the Dunedin area by winter 1999.

Mainland Brewery (DB Breweries)

ADDRESS Sheffield Street, Washdyke, Timaru **PHONE** (03) 633 2059 **FAX** (03) 688 2225 **BREWER** Nick Duncan

Mainland Brewery is a joint venture between DB Breweries and eight South Island licensing trusts. It was built to meet the demand for DB beers in the south and the green-fields site at Washdyke, near Timaru, was ideally located for servicing the trusts' hotels and taverns. At the time there was much debate whether to build a conventional batch-fermentation brewery or use the revolutionary continuous-fermentation process developed by Morton Coutts in the 1950s. Directors opted for continuous fermentation, which allows a constant flow of ingredients through the brewery, producing beer 24 hours a day to a consistent quality at a lower cost than batch-brewing. While other DB Breweries products are brewed at Mainland, it is DB Draught for which it is best known. This beer is available throughout the country.

DB Draught 4% abv

A crystal-clear copper-gold in colour, this beer has a perfumey malt aroma with both sweet-fruit and mild-hop influences. The texture is moderately creamy with a clean, refreshing appeal. Full malt flavours dominate at first — these become more raisiny on the middle palate. It has a generous mouth-feel that takes the residual sweetness on to the finish. An honest rendition of the Kiwi brown-beer style, popular with traditionalists, this beer will feel at home with no-nonsense fare such as meat pies, hearty steaks, roasts and casseroles.

Wanaka Beerworks

ADDRESS SH 6, RD 2 Wanaka **PHONE** (03) 443 1865 **FAX** (03) 443 1862 **E-MAIL** wanaka.beer.works@xtra.co.nz **BREWERS** Dave Gillies & Brian Cope **OPEN** 9 am–6 pm Mon–Sat

Wanaka Beerworks is situated next to the Wanaka Transport Museum, about seven minutes' drive from Wanaka township. It is the dream child of Sky and Dave Gillies. Working with

FACT Some sources claim that, after consuming a bucket or two of the vibrant brew they called *aul,* or ale, the Vikings would head fearlessly into battle, often without armour or even shirts. In fact, the term 'berserk' means 'bareshirt' in Norse.

fellow brewer Brian Cope they follow a European philosophy of brewing. Adhering to the Reinheitsgebot (the Bavarian beer purity law of 1516), this unique brewery offers an entirely natural, hand-crafted product. The impressively packaged products are available in liquor stores throughout Central Otago, and in local pubs such as the Kingsway and the Luggate Arms in Wanaka, and the Briar & Thyme in Alexandra.

Brewski 4.8% abv
Wheat-gold in colour, when poured this beer offers a thick, creamy, white head. The aroma is grassy with citrus fruit and honey flavours in evidence as well. There is plenty of body in this creamy beer and it tastes of honey and malt with a well-balanced hop bitterness on the back palate. It will be enjoyed as an aperitif — or try it with pizza or an antipasto platter so you can experience the different levels of flavour.

Tall Black 5.2% abv
This is a dark brown-black beer with a thick, creamy head. Served at room temperature for total enjoyment, it has an aroma that is strongly caramel with a slightly mealiness as well. The texture is lighter than the colour might suggest and it is fresh and clean in the mouth. The flavours are complex, with chocolate, caramel and toffee all in evidence. The slightly higher alcohol content adds weight and a

little dryness to the beer and gives it yet another dimension. Enjoy it as is or with fruit desserts.

McNeills Cottage Brewery

ADDRESS 14 Church Street, Queenstown **PHONE** (03) 442 9688
BREWER Steve Hagerty **OPEN** 11.30 am–late daily

In 1993 Steve Hagerty and partner Paul Graf established McNeills Cottage Brewery as a brew-pub within a historic stone building in the centre of Queenstown. Brewer Steve's intention is to offer a unique alternative for the local beer drinkers and McNeills presently offers their own brews in the bar on site and supplies five other outlets within the Queenstown area.

Moonlight Ale 4.2% abv
This copper-gold ale has a lightly malted, sweet-fruit aroma and a mealy, toasted-malt flavour. Popular as a mainstream light-lager style, it is a good summer quaffer for barbecue or beach.

Classic Black 4.2% abv
A popular choice in the winter, this brown-black unfiltered beer has a fruity, caramel aroma. Its texture is light and fresh and it has a fruit-syrup flavour with additional chocolate and toasted-malt characters. On the back palate it has a slight malt bitterness, but overall it is a mainstream dark beer that can be enjoyed on its own around a warm fire or in other seasons with fresh raw oysters.

Wakatipu Gold Lager 4.2% abv
Made with Nelson hops, this pale straw lager has light hop aromas with a hint of citrus. It is light and easy-drinking, clean and fresh.

When served ice cold it has a broad appeal with no significant aftertaste. Like others in its style, this beer will partner curry and spicy food well.

Duff's Brewery

ADDRESS 695 Great King Street, Dunedin **PHONE & FAX** (03) 477 7276
BREWER Gavin Duff **OPEN** 11 am–8 pm Mon–Sat

After many years working as a mechanic, Gavin Duff opted for a change in lifestyle, opened a brewery and now produces beers designed to appeal to the average Kiwi brown-beer drinker. Duff's Brewery has been operating in Dunedin's Great King Street since August 1997. Duff's beers are available throughout Central Otago and Southland, in some cafés in Dunedin, and from the brewery itself.

Duffs Special Draught 4% abv

This light brown beer has a very slight hop aroma. The mouth-feel is good, with a distinctly grassy flavour and a hint of spiciness. It is a lightweight beer with low flavour levels, appealing to those looking for a good quaffer — try it with grilled marinated steak.

Duffs Classic Gold Wheat Lager 4% abv

Pale straw in colour, this is another lightweight beer in the lager style. The aroma is definite wheat/barley — freshly baled hay also comes to mind. It has a good, solid mouth-feel and a medium degree of carbonation that comes from conditioning and a top-up of carbonation after fermentation. The finish is crisp and clean, and once again the strong wheat influences are to the fore. It is best drunk as an aperitif.

Duffs Edinburgh Draught Ale 4% abv

An interesting burnt-orange tinge makes this an attractive beer in the glass, especially when well poured with a substantial, creamy head. It has a strong aroma of hops and the hop bitterness comes through in the taste as well. It has a dry finish with a lingering bitterness that will be attractive to some. Easy to drink as a session beer, it would also be good with meat off the grill.

Duffs Dark Ale 4% abv

This is a dark beer, almost black in colour, with a distinctive wheaty smell about it. Lighter in texture than expected, it is best drunk at room temperature. The flavour brings to mind iced coffee, with only a slight fruitiness. In fact coffee lovers are sure to enjoy this offering, and for something different I would serve it with home-made ginger slice.

Meenan Wines & Spirits

ADDRESS 670 Great King Street, Dunedin **PHONE** (03) 477 2047 **FAX** (03) 477 2049 **BREWER** Stuart Littlejohn **OPEN** 8.30 am–6 pm Mon–Fri, 8.30 am–7 pm Sat

Established as a family business venture in June 1997, this brewery is part of a retail liquor outlet, carrying the same name, in the heart of Dunedin. Head brewer Stuart Littlejohn aims to produce beers that will appeal to a wide audience of local beer drinkers. Supplying pubs and clubs throughout Central Otago and Southland, Meenan's has a strong local following eager to drink reasonably priced alternatives to mainstream New Zealand beers. The range is available from Meenan Wines & Spirits.

Meenan Lager 5% abv
Pale gold to straw in colour, this highly carbonated, lightweight beer in the lager style has a honey and hop aroma that is also slightly yeasty. It is smooth and crisp with a characteristic hint of citrus from the Halletau hops used in its production. A sweet finish means it will be a good quaffing beer to refresh the palate after spicy food.

Meenan Finest Best Bitter 3.8% abv
Dark copper with a good, creamy head, this beer shines when drunk at just under room temperature. There is an easily discernible smoky peat aroma that comes through in the flavour. With little hop flavour evident, the malt provides a hint of sweet coffee, especially on the middle palate, while adding an interesting dryness. The flavour fades quickly, making it an easy-drinking beer ideal for accommodating a variety of beer preferences. It would be perfect for barbecues.

Meenan High Country Draught 4% abv
Another mainstream offering, the High Country Draught is dark chocolate in colour and has a reasonably strong hop aroma. It has well-rounded texture — smooth and with plenty of body, in the style of an English ale. Toasted malts have been added, so there is a bitter-sweet element to this beer that means it makes good drinking with red meat. Try it with biltong or smoked beef jerky.

Meenan Extra Strong Ale 5% abv
My favourite from the Meenan selection, this dark, almost black beer is rich but not perhaps as creamy as expected. Rather it is crisp and clean and can be enjoyed well chilled. The aroma is yeasty with toasted malt characters, and this comes through as a roasted, almost burnt-toast flavour and a rather dry finish. I would be tempted to serve this interesting offering with a strong cheese — stilton perhaps.

Speight's Brewery (New Zealand Breweries)

ADDRESS 200 Rattray Street, Dunedin **PHONE** (03) 477 9480 **FAX** (03) 477 9489 **TOURS** 10.30 am Mon–Thu and by arrangement

Established in 1876 and located in the heart of Dunedin, Speight's Brewery is part of the New Zealand Breweries group of companies and survives with much fascinating history and a very stable work force. The locals are fiercely loyal to Speight's products and the brewery returns the compliment by being an active partner in many local and provincial community activities. Speight's beers have over recent years gained some popularity outside of the brewery's home region but nowhere are they more popular than in Dunedin, South Canterbury and Southland. These beers all have their own character. They are mainstream, with broad appeal, but also have something a little extra, which is no doubt what endears them to lovers of the classic beer styles. Speight's Brewery's products are widely available throughout the country in both packaged and draught form.

Speight's Gold Medal Ale 4% abv

The 'Pride of the South' has been brewed in Dunedin since 1876, supplying the palate preferences of what has come to be known as the 'southern man'. Copper-gold in colour, this beer has plenty of malt sweetness in the aroma as well as some grassiness. It is a fresh bouquet. The texture too is light and clean, and the flavour, in keeping with the aroma, is malty with medium sweetness, slightly mealy and with reasonably grassy notes as well. There is plenty of finish — overall it is a well-balanced brew with broad appeal. A good choice with meat dishes, it would be superb with more gamey variants such as venison, duck and rabbit.

Speight's Distinction Ale 5% abv

The 115th anniversary of Speight's was commemorated with the aptly named Distinction Ale. Intended as a single-batch brew, it proved so popular its production was continued. It has a dark copper hue with a tinge of red and a thick, creamy head. It's quite fruity on the nose with some esters evident. The texture is crisp and clean and there is plenty of mouth-feel. The full flavour is a good balance of malt and hop, with hints of caramel and butterscotch. There is good length and a mild, pleasantly dry aftertaste. It holds its own with any full-flavoured main course. Try it with a favourite casserole.

Speight's Old Dark Malt Ale 4% abv

The colour of this beer is a lovely dark brown with a red hue, the aroma full of malt with dark chocolate, butterscotch and caramel influences. The texture is luscious and full, with lots of body. Rich malt and fruit flavours prevail in the flavour, which is not as sweet as you might expect and is balanced by the hop bitterness. It is fresh and clean with good length and a touch of dryness on the back palate to keep it interesting. Like all the Speight's range it will go well with red meat, but I would recommend drinking it with a hot, rich dessert such as steamed pudding with clotted cream.

The Emerson Brewing Company

ADDRESS 4 Grange Street, Dunedin **PHONE** (03) 477 1812 **BREWER** Richard Emerson **OPEN** noon–2 pm & 4 pm–6 pm Mon–Sat

Travelling through the UK and Europe, Richard Emerson came to love the huge variety of fuller-flavoured beers he found there. Richard's objective is to produce similar beers, true to style, that will appeal to the palates of fine-beer drinkers in

New Zealand. Along the way he aims to further educate the Kiwi beer drinker to appreciate the diversity in beer styles. The Emerson Brewing Company has been operating since 1992 and has earned a large band of followers all over the country. Richard's efforts have also attracted favourable comments on more than one occasion from Michael Jackson, the world's foremost beer writer. Emerson's beers can be purchased direct from the brewery and are widely available in liquor stores throughout Otago, as well as in Christchurch and as far north as Kaikoura. A selection can also be found in the beautifully refurbished Criterion Hotel in Oamaru. Be sure to ask Richard if he has any special brews he is willing to let you try! By the way, Emerson's beers are also available by mail order.

Emerson's 1812 India Pale Ale 4.9% abv

Brown-gold in colour with a rich aroma of spring grass and a hint of malt sweetness, this beer is mouth-filling with a true hop bitterness that gives the middle/back palate a wake-up call. It's robust enough to accompany red-meat dishes, especially those with earthy flavours.

Emerson's Pilsener 4.4% abv

This beer is lime-gold with a delicate aroma of herbs and spices. With slight carbonation resulting from filtration, this organic pilsener has a gentle maltiness with a mild bitterness. A fresh, crisp offering with a good hoppy finish, it is a complex but well-balanced beer with lovely lager characteristics. It will partner any spicy Asian food, as well as full-flavoured pasta dishes.

Emerson's Weissbier Hefe-Weizenbier 4.8% abv

Drinkers not familiar with wheat beers should not allow themselves to be put off by the cloudy character of this award-winning offering.

Pale gold with a distinct aroma of Juicyfruit chewing gum, it is crisp and clean with a lingering tropical-fruit flavour balanced by a slight hop astringency. It needs to be at room temperature to be fully appreciated, and makes great drinking as an aperitif or with blue cheese.

Emerson's Bookbinder Bitter 3.7% abv

Dark copper in colour, this true bitter has a gentle aroma reminiscent of blackcurrant with a touch of yeastiness. It pours with a lovely, lingering head. The texture is creamy and rich with a mild refined graininess. It has a comparatively low alcohol content and a full, malty flavour, and surprises at the end with a dash of citrus just to keep the palate fresh. It is a complex beer best served before a meal or as a partner to hearty meat dishes.

Emerson's Weissbier Dunkel 4.8% abv

The colour of dark chocolate, this beer has an amazing aroma of banana lumps, stonefruit and hazelnuts! It is smooth, crisp and mouth-filling with a complex flavour profile, at times slightly yeasty and slightly sweet with a wine-like off-dry finish. It's a good beer to serve guests at your next barbecue or with snacks during the rugby on telly!

Emerson's Whisky Porter 4.9% abv

A once-a-year brew, this quirky little number is a winner with both beer lovers and members of whisky appreciation societies. It is made by ageing Emerson's Porter for three months in spent whisky casks from the local distillery. It has a rich, dark brown colour and a whisky and slightly peppery aroma. Peaty, smoky flavours permeate the malt and smooth cold-coffee aftertaste. It is deep, dark and delicious with smoked fish pie or duck risotto.

Emerson's 'Old 95' 7% abv

The colour of golden syrup, with a red tint, this beer has an aroma that conjures up memories of Mum's steamed pudding. It has a rich, creamy texture with a big, buxom mouth-feel. A slightly burnt flavour (not the same toastiness as toasted malt) and a hint of orange and definite fruitcake characters dominate. Great on its own, it would also pair well with any game meat and gutsy gravy.

Emerson's London Porter 4.9% abv

Almost black in the bottle, this true-to-style porter pours as a very dark brown beer with plenty of fruity aroma and a creamy texture. It is a 'big' beer with lots of character. Its gentle hop bitterness is balanced by an equal weight of maltiness. The alcohol comes through too, doing its part by giving the beer some extra kick right at the end. It is another complex and full-flavoured offering to be enjoyed equally well with lamb roasts and meat pies.

Other New Zealand breweries

Unfortunately no information on these breweries was available at the time of writing.

Twin Pines Brew House
Address: Haruru Falls, Paihia
Brewer: Martin Allen

Petone Brewery
Address: 340 Jackson Street, Petone, Lower Hutt, Wellington
Phone & fax: (04) 568 8481
Brewer: Manfred Graff

Milkshed Brewing Company
Address: Cnr Davidsons & Greenpark Roads, RD 4 Greenpark, Christchurch
Phone: (03) 325 5711
Brewer: Nigel Gerard

Wests Cordials
135 Bayview Road, Dunedin
Phone: (03) 455 4458; Fax: (03) 455 4445
Brewer: Alistair Stoddart

New Zealand beer labels

One of the things we do really well in New Zealand, apart from making beer, is branding it. For some it is an intrinsic part of the marketing process; for others it is simply part of the passion and the craftmanship. There is a huge range of designs included here yet not all beers are represented. Some beers are served only on tap and so have no label as such. Some brewers chose to submit only a sample of their range; others were in the process of redesigning their labels.

The following pages offer a treasure trove of labels: plain and extravagant, complex and simple, multi coloured and black and white. Some celebrate the regional character of the beer and some the idiosyncratic nature of the brewer. In order to include as many as possible the labels have not been printed to a common scale. They are set out in the same order as the tasting notes in the book.

Hokianga Breweries
p 18

Northland Breweries
p 18

Northland Breweries
p 18

Northland Breweries
p 18

Burkes Kaipara Brewery
p 19

Burkes Kaipara Brewery
p 20

Burkes Kaipara Brewery
p 20

Pilot Bay Brewing Co.
p 21

Pilot Bay Brewing Co.
p 21

Pilot Bay Brewing Co.
p 21

Pilot Bay Brewing Co.
p 22

Pilot Bay Brewing Co.
p 22

Waiheke Island Microbrewery
p 23

Waiheke Island Microbrewery
p 23

Waiheke Island Microbrewery
p 24

Rangitoto Brewing Co.
p 25

Rangitoto Brewing Co.
p 26

Rangitoto Brewing Co.
p 26

Rangitoto Brewing Co.
p 26

Rangitoto Brewing Co.
p 27

Brofords Beers
p 28

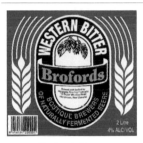

Brofords Beers
p 28

Brofords Beers
p 28

Brofords Beers
p 28

Brofords Beers
p 29

Bean Rock Brewing Co.
p 30

The Loaded Hog Brewery
p 31

The Loaded Hog Brewery
p 31

The Loaded Hog Brewery
p 31

The Loaded Hog Brewery
p 32

Shakespeare Tavern & Brewery
p 35

Lion Breweries
p 37

Lion Breweries
p 37

Lion Breweries
p 38

Lion Breweries
p 38

Lion Breweries
p 38

Lion Breweries
p 39

Lion Breweries
p 39

Lion Breweries
p 39

Galbraith Brewing Co.
p 40

Galbraith Brewing Co.
p 41

Galbraith Brewing Co.
p 41

Australis Brewing Co.
p 42

Australis Brewing Co.
p 43

Australis Brewing Co.
p 43

Onehunga Spring Brewery
p 46

Onehunga Spring Brewery
p 46

Onehunga Spring Brewery
p 47

Onehunga Spring Brewery
p 47

Onehunga Spring Brewery
p 47

Waitemata Brewery
p 49

Waitemata Brewery
p 49

Waitemata Brewery
p 49

Waitemata Brewery
p 49

Waitemata Brewery
p 50

Waitemata Brewery
p 50

Waitemata Brewery
p 50

Auckland Breweries
p 52

Auckland Breweries
p 52

Auckland Breweries
p 52

Auckland Breweries
p 53

Steam Brewing Co.
p 54

Steam Brewing Co.
p 55

Independent Brewery
p 56

Independent Brewery
p 57

Kahikatea Brewery
p 58

Kahikatea Brewery
p 58

Kahikatea Brewery
p 58

Kahikatea Brewery
p 59

Sunshine Brewing Co.
p 60

Sunshine Brewing Co.
p 60

Sunshine Brewing Co.
p 60

Sunshine Brewing Co.
p 60

Sunshine Brewing Co.
p 61

Brew Haus
p 63

White Cliffs Brewing Co.
p 64

O'Neills Brewing Co.
p 64

O'Neills Brewing Co.
p 65

O'Neills Brewing Co.
p 65

Coastal Breweries
p 66

Independent Brewery
p 67

Independent Brewery
p 67

Roosters Brewhouse
p 68

Roosters Brewhouse
p 69

Roosters Brewhouse
p 69

Roosters Brewhouse
p 69

Roosters Brewhouse
p 70

Tui Brewery
p 74

Burridges Brewery
p 75

Burridges Brewery
p 75

Burridges Brewery
p 75

Parrot & Jigger
p 76

Parrot & Jigger
p 77

Parrot & Jigger
p 77

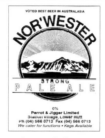

Parrot & Jigger
p 77

Parrot & Jigger
p 77

Polar Brewery
p 78

Polar Brewery
p 79

Polar Brewery
p 79

Polar Brewery
p 79

Mussel Inn
p 83

Mussel Inn
p 84

Mussel Inn
p 84

Mussel Inn
p 84

Mussel Inn
p 84

Lighthouse Brewery
p 86

Lighthouse Brewery
p 86

Lighthouse Brewery
p 86

Nelson Bays Brewery
p 87

Nelson Bays Brewery
p 87

Nelson Bays Brewery
p 88

Nelson Bays Brewery
p 88

Harrington's Brewery
p 89

Harrington's Brewery
p 89

Harrington's Brewery
p 90

Harrington's Brewery
p 90

Harrington's Brewery
p 90

Roc Mac
p 91

Roc Mac
p 92

Roc Mac
p 92

Roc Mac
p 92

Roc Mac
p 93

Roc Mac
p 93

Marlborough Brewing Co.
p 94

Marlborough Brewing Co.
p 94

Marlborough
Brewing Co. p 94

Marlborough
Brewing Co. p 95

Renwick Breweries
p 96

Renwick Breweries
p 96

Renwick Breweries
p 96

Renwick Breweries
p 97

Pink Elephant Brewery
p 98

Pink Elephant Brewery
p 98

Pink Elephant Brewery
p 98

Pink Elephant Brewery
p 99

Miner's Brewery
p 100

Miner's Brewery
p 100

Miner's Brewery
p 101

Monteith's Brewing Co.
p 102

Monteith's Brewing Co.
p 102

Monteith's Brewing Co.
p 102

Monteith's Brewing Co.
p 103

Monteith's Brewing Co.
p 103

Monteith's Brewing Co.
p 103

Monteith's Brewing Co.
p 104

Kaiapoi Brewery
p 105

Kaiapoi Brewery
p 105

Dux de Lux
p 106

Dux de Lux
p 106

Dux de Lux
p 106

Dux de Lux
p 107

Dux de Lux
p 107

Dux de Lux
p 107

Canterbury Independent
Brewery p 108

Canterbury Independent
Brewery p 108

Canterbury Independent
Brewery p 109

Canterbury Independent
Brewery p 109

Canterbury Independent
Brewery p 109

Canterbury Brewery
p 110

Harrington's Brewery
p 112

Harrington's Brewery
p 113

Harrington's Brewery
p 113

Harrington's Brewery
p 113

Harrington's Brewery
p 113

Harrington's Brewery
p 114

Harrington's Brewery
p 114

Mainland Brewery
p 117

Wanaka Beerworks
p 118

Wanaka Beerworks
p 118

McNeills Cottage Brewery
p 119

Duff's Brewery
p 120

Duff's Brewery
p 121

Duff's Brewery
p 121

Meenan Wines & Spirits
p 122

Meenan Wines & Spirits
p 122

Meenan Wines & Spirits
p 122

Meenan Wines & Spirits
p 122

Speight's Brewery
p 123

Speight's Brewery
p 124

Speight's Brewery
p 124

The Emerson Brewing Co.
p 125

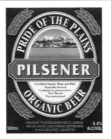

The Emerson Brewing Co.
p 125

The Emerson Brewing Co.
p 125

The Emerson Brewing Co.
p 126

The Emerson Brewing Co.
p 127

The Emerson Brewing Co.
p 127

Imported beers

The New Zealand beer consumer is well served when it comes to imported beer. More than 100 brews from all around the world are available and the list is growing weekly. In recent years improved means of packing and distribution have resulted in imported product arriving here in much better condition. Growing popularity also means greater turnover and so the product you purchase should be fresher.

Following is a listing of beers I have tasted by country of origin. Not all retail outlets stock all the imported beers, and some are available only at restaurants. However the list does provide a good indication of what is currently being brought into the country.

Australia

Carlton Cold Filtered Bitter 4.9% abv
Pale straw, full-strength beer with crisp texture, good bodyweight and a hop bitterness on the palate. There is melon and tropical fruit in the flavour as well. Good balance and lengthy finish.

Carlton Stripe 4.0% abv
Mid-straw brown with a distinctly hop aroma. The mouth-feel is

generous, the texture crisp and clean. The bitterness comes through in the taste, which has some herb and spice notes as well. A pleasantly long aftertaste.

Cascade Premium Lager 5.2% abv

A distinctive aroma and a crisp, clean texture that is consistent to the finish. Generous hopping shows on a palate that is full of flavour, including some subtle floral notes.

Cooper's Premium Clear Ale 4.9% abv

A yellow-gold colour, a good creamy head and a mild hop aroma introduce this beer, which has a rounded and full-bodied palate of moderate bitterness. There is good mouth-feel and a moderate malt and hop finish.

Cooper's Sparkling Ale 5.8% abv

Brewed using the top-fermentation method, this product displays a solid head and distinctive, full-bodied flavour enhanced by a soft, fruity character and a sediment that gives a cloudy appearance.

Cooper's Best Extra Stout 6.8% abv

Cooper's Best Extra Stout, also brewed using the top-fermentation method, is a good example of the robust, full-flavoured stout family. The unique, rich, dark texture of the product is produced by specially roasted black malt.

Cooper's Original Pale Ale 4.5% abv

Fermented in the 'Burton-on-Trent' style, this product is made in the same way as Cooper's Sparkling Ale, with a full, fruity flavour. Secondary fermentation produces a fine, cloudy residue in the finished product.

Diamond 4.2% abv

A full-flavoured, golden grain-coloured beer with fewer calories than regular beer. The aroma is sweet and grassy, the texture lightweight and refreshing. Flavourful with a caramel finish.

Foster's Lager 4.9% abv

A light-coloured lager style with a slightly hoppy but yeasty/malty nose. The flavour has full malt character with balanced, clean, hop bitterness. Crisp and clean texture with good mouth-feel and length.

Foster's Light 2.5% abv

Foster's Light has only half the alcohol content of its famous parent. Its full malt character and clean hop bitterness are combined with a delicate estery, yeasty and malty nose to produce a low-alcohol beer of excellent length.

Foster's Special Bitter 2.8% abv

A refreshing, full-bodied, low-alcohol beer that's brewed with extra hops to give a welcome bitter flavour that is consistent from start to finish.

Power's Bitter 4.8% abv

This Queensland beer has a strong hop tang balanced by a sweet palate and is quite refreshing when chilled.

Resch's Pilsener 4.6% abv

Traditional pilsener with cut-grass and spice aroma and a smooth palate, followed by a distinct dry, hoppy finish.

Swan Special Light 0.9% abv

Produced from fully brewed regular-strength beer using a vacuum distillation process. Almost all of the alcohol is extracted but the character and taste of the beer is kept. It is crisp, clean and distinctly bitter — and it has only half the calories of the average beer.

Tooheys Blue Label 2.5% abv

Tooheys Blue Label is made using a high proportion of flavoured crystal malt, mashed at higher temperature than normal. This ensures good texture and body. Specially selected hops finish the flavour on a crisp, dry note.

Victoria Bitter 4.9% abv

Well-balanced fruity/malty and yeasty notes in the aroma. The full malt and increased clean hop bitterness is complemented by a pleasant sweetness on the palate. It has a stronger, drier finish.

Belgium

Belle Vue Kriek 5.2% abv

Ruby-red with strong cherry aroma and fruity, sweet taste carried by a clean and crisp texture that fills the palate. Very distinctive flavour from start to finish. Some dryness around the sides of the mouth.

Belle Vue Framboise 5.2% abv

Made from wheat, lambic and raspberries. Pink colour; strong aroma; fruity, sweet taste. Lengthy, pervasive, sweet aftertaste, somewhat medicinal.

Belle Vue Gueuze 5.2% abv

Made from wheat and over-aged hops, showing golden colour. Full-bodied taste with good balance between sweet, bitter and sour influences. Good length.

Chimay Red Trappist Ale 7% abv

Definite pink blush; soft creamy aroma with good level of hops. Gentle fruit in mouth; long, bitter finish. Bottle conditioned.

Chimay White Trappist Ale 8% abv

Pale peach in colour; dry, firm, hoppy aroma; full of flavour with lots of fruit sweetness on the palate. Will become drier on cellaring.

Chimay Blue Trappist Ale 9% abv

Redcurrant fruit and hops aroma; fruity palate; lingering fruit and sherry notes in finish. Very spicy.

Duvel Top Fermented Strong Beer 8.5% abv

'Doovil' means 'devil' in Flemish. Light fruit and hop aroma; pear-like fruit in mouth; long bitter-sweet finish with developing hop bitterness towards the finish.

Hoegaarden White 5% abv

Unfiltered, refermented beer; natural cloudy appearance; coriander and curacao complement its refreshing sour-sweet taste and fruity, soft bitter aroma. Moderately smooth and mouth-filling. Bottle conditioned.

Hoegaarden Grand Cru 8.7% abv

Hazy, softly golden colour with a subtle, complex flavour, strong aroma tending toward sweet and delicately hoppy. Creamy texture with plenty of length. Bottle conditioned.

Hoegaarden Forbidden Fruit 8.8% abv

Dark red, complex beer brewed with dark malts; well balanced, soft and dry at the same time. Bottle conditioned.

Leffe Blonde 6.6% abv
A sunny, golden-yellow colour complements a taste that is aromatic, full bodied with delicate sweetness and balanced flavour.

Stella Artois 5.2% abv
Pilsener-style beer with a refined dryness. It has a very firm body, a crisp, hoppy finish and a full aroma that exhibits, as does the palate, some spicy flavours. Well balanced with pleasant aftertaste.

Canada

Labatts Blue 5% abv
A fragrant lager with a pleasing golden colour and mellow smoothness which indicates a low bitterness level for very accessible drinking.

Moosehead 5% abv
Clean, crisp sparkling lager with malty undertones and a pleasing sweetness on the palate.

China

Tsing Tao 4.5% abv
Tawny-yellow colour; malt nose; malt and hop flavour. Good body, medium-dry malt finish and aftertaste with plenty of hop backing.

Zhujiang Beer 3.8–4.3% abv
Very pale gold with a nutty and grassy aroma. The texture is crisp and clean. An easy-to-drink lager style with plenty of hop flavours and some cut-hay character as well.

Czech Republic

Budejovicky Budvar 5% abv

Gentle hops and toffee-malt aromas; superb balance of malt and hops in the mouth. It has a bitter-sweet finish with light vanilla hops.

Pilsner Urquell 4.1% abv

Golden colour with a slight lime hue; mild, grassy, hop aroma; full, dry flavour; good length; hop-bitter finish.

Denmark

Carlsberg Green 5% abv

This is a stylish gold-coloured lager with a good body and a vinous character. A typical European-style lager with strong flavour intensity coming from malty, fruity flavours. Excellent mouth-feel and generous length.

Elephant Beer 7.2% abv

A rich, golden-amber, full-strength beer with some yeasty aromas and an unusually big, fruity palate. At the same time strong, malty flavours are balanced with moderately bitter hops and a slight sweetness. The extra strength of Elephant Beer makes it worthy of respect.

Giraf Gold 5.6% abv

A richly coloured, smooth-textured beer exhibiting bitter-sweet characteristics on the nose and palate. It has some spice flavours as well. A refreshing aftertaste makes this an interesting food beer.

Tuborg Gold 5.5% abv
Straw-gold in colour; light, clean texture and good mouth-feel. The flavour is full with a good balance of malt and hops. Finishes quickly.

France

Kronenbourg 5% abv
A soft, grainy nose with a subtle, light hoppiness. A light, well-rounded flavour with hop and straw influences. Excellent hop bitterness to finish.

Germany

Becks 5% abv
A fresh, malty lager with a hoppy tang. The flavour is rich and complex. The texture is full and the finish long.

Bitburger Premium 4.6% abv
Pale gold colour; light, dry with pronounced hop flavour overriding soft maltiness in middle palate; finishes with subtle, elegant bitterness.

Holsten Premium 5.2% abv
Assertive hoppiness and dryness, rounded malty character. Good length.

Kostritzer Schwarzbier 4.8% abv
Dark-roast malt, chocolate and hops aromas; bitter chocolate in the mouth; big finish packaged with dark fruit chocolate and hops.

Lowenbrau Original 5.2% abv
Lively, citric aroma; fine balance of malt and hops in the mouth; a long finish packed with hop bitterness.

Raunchenfelser Steinbier 4.9% abv

Stone-brewed beer. Top-fermented with a fine, smoky, caramelised flavour from the immersion of red-hot stones in the brewing vessel.

Romerkrug 'Stein' 4.9% abv

Fine champagne-like sparkle, good malt flavour and creamy head. Texture is crisp and clean with good mouth-feel and a sweetish finish.

Schneider Weiss Beer (helle) Original 5.4% abv

Complex bouquet of banana, cloves and nutmeg, tart fruit in the mouth and creamy, fruity finish with hints of bubble gum.

Schneider Aventinus Weiss Doppelbock 8% abv

Bronze-red; rich spice and chocolate aroma on palate; more spices, vinous fruit and cloves in the finish. Generous mouth-feel.

Street Pauli Girl 5% abv

Full flavoured, with a wheaty, light and grainy character. Light hop and straw aroma. It shows a clean, fresh palate and a light and crisp texture with a character of style and balance. Good length.

Warsteiner Premium 4.8% abv

Bright pale gold in colour, with a very hoppy aroma and a complex malt and hop flavour. Excellent balance, big hop finish and a long, dry hop aftertaste.

India

Flying Horse Royal Lager 4% abv

Pale yellow-gold; grassy aroma that shows a bit of treacle; crisp and lightweight; very mild and sweet with short length and a drier finish.

Kalyani Export Special 4.8% abv

Yellow-gold with a lime hue, this beer has no discernible aroma and a lightweight mouth-feel. The texture is clean, the flavour grassy and a little fruity. No length and a crisp finish.

Kingfisher Premium Lager 5% abv

Yellow-gold with a yellow tint. Hoppy aroma with a bubble-gum note. Crisp and clean, the flavour has both malt and hop character. Lightweight overall and easy-drinking.

Ireland

Beamish Red Ale 4.5% abv

With a distinctive chestnut-red hue and a creamy, smooth mouth-feel, this beer has a distinct hop aroma and an exceptional malt/hop balance in the flavour. A full-bodied Irish ale with full and lengthy aftertaste, best enjoyed well chilled.

Beamish Irish Stout 4.2% abv

Dark, almost black, this stout has a distinct hop aroma. The texture is smooth and refreshing, the flavour rich and mouth-filling with strong chocolate and roast malt characters. An appealing finish and plenty of length.

FACT In English pubs, ale is ordered by pints and quarts. So in old England, when customers got unruly, the bartender would yell at them to mind their own pints and quarts and settle down. Some experts say that's where we get the phrase 'mind your p's and q's'.

Murphy's Irish Stout 4% abv

Smooth and creamy dark brown stout from the Lady's Well Brewery in Cork. Roasted-coffee aroma; medium-heavy body and roasted flavour with chocolate accents; dry finish.

Italy

Peroni Nastro Azzuro 5.2% abv

A clean and fresh, hoppy nose with some yeasty aroma. A full, crisp palate and residual hop bitterness. Well balanced with good flavour.

Jamaica

Red Stripe Lager 4.7% abv

Dark golden colour; smooth sweetness; malty mellow style contributed to by use of Yakima hops.

Japan

Asahi Super Dry 5% abv

This dry Asian beer is one of the best of its type. Asahi invented the dry-brewing process where not all the grain is malted. Distinctive; crisp and dry; light hop flavour; best served cold.

Kirin 4.5% abv

Highly aromatic and highly flavoured (leathery, flavour of wet paper), plenty of length. Kirin is a fully hopped beer with loads of taste. It is a lager of substance, clean and well balanced.

Sapporo Premium Lager 4.5% abv

Grainy aroma; malty in the mouth; dry finish with some hop notes.

Korea

Hite Beer 4.5% abv
Hazy pale gold; light malt and hop nose; light, dry, faint, hop flavour; some faint sweetness in the finish. Light body with a slight dry-malt aftertaste.

Mexico

Corona Extra 4.6% abv
A hoppy nose with a tinge of cornmeal and a slightly yeasty, maize character. Texture is crisp and dry, with a powerful initial taste of sweet malt and hop. It is a simple and refreshing beer with a light gold colour and fruity palate.

Sol 4.1% abv
A popular summer beer, light straw in colour with negligible aroma. The texture is lightweight and fizzy. Flavour is dry with cornmeal characteristics. Unusual and quite enjoyable.

Namibia

Tafel Lager 4% abv
Pale straw-gold in colour with a floral/perfumed aroma. The texture is creamy with good mouth-feel and medium body. The flavour has hints of tropical fruit over the top of the malt sweetness. Some hop bitterness towards the end provides a crisp finish.

Windhoek Lager 4% abv
Straw-gold with both malt and hop in the aroma. Texture is crisp and clean with generous mouth-feel. The flavour is malty sweet with

some dryness on the sides of the palate suggesting hop. It's light, mildly bitter and refreshing at the end.

Windhoek Light 2% abv
Pale gold in colour with mild aroma and flavour. On the nose slightly grainy and musty. The texture is lightweight and crisp. Some malt sweetness and melon and citrus notes as well. Short finish leaving a clean aftertaste.

The Netherlands

Grolsch 5% abv
Internationally recognised for its unique 473-millilitre swing-top bottle with the porcelain stopper, Grolsch is a pale lager with a light, well-rounded body complete with a hint of malt sweetness.

Oranjeboom Premium Lager 5% abv
Elegant beer with full flavour, mildly bitter, showing golden colour.

Singapore

ABC Stout 8% abv
Opaque brown head; off-dry malt and hop nose. The palate is complex, herbal roasted-malt flavour until the finish that is dry and faintly burnt. Long, off-dry, malt aftertaste with some liquorice and molasses.

Anchor Pilsener Beer 5% abv
Deep gold; hop and malt nose; slightly roasted-malt flavour; malt hop finish; decent balance with good body; long malt and hop aftertaste.

FACT It is claimed that many years ago in England, pub frequenters had a whistle baked into the rim or handle of their ceramic cups. When they needed a refill they used the whistle to get some service. 'Wet your whistle' is the phrase inspired by this practice.

Raffles Lager 4.5% abv
A light straw-coloured, tropical brew with a fruity aroma and a full, smooth mouth-feel. A moderately sweet flavour and some dryness on the back palate. Good length.

Tiger 5% abv
Pale yellow-gold with a mild aroma and slightly syrupy texture. The flavour is mild and clean with a high level of sweetness and a trace of hop bitterness.

South Africa

Bavaria 'Edel' Lager 5% abv
Lime-gold in colour with a good head, this beer has no discernible aroma. The texture is crisp and dry and fairly complex. The flavour is full with grassy/grainy characters and a nice hop/malt balance. A good finish with plenty of aftertaste.

Castle Lager 5% abv
Very pale gold with a moderately hoppy aroma with some straw influences as well. The texture is crisp and clean with good mouth-weight. On the palate it is refreshingly hoppy with a hop bitterness balanced by some fruity sweetness on the finish. Good drinking.

Kaltenberg 'Royal' Lager 5% abv

Pale yellow-gold with a malty, sweet-fruit aroma. It is smooth with lots of body, while the flavour has molasses and treacley influences and a good hop balance. There is plenty of length, a bitter-sweet finish and an off-dry aftertaste. Classy lager.

Thailand

Singha 5.9% abv

Mid-straw in colour with a moderate aroma of malt and hops. The texture is rich and quite weighty, somewhat oily. The flavour is mild with bitter-sweet influences. Reasonable length with a sweetish finish.

Turkey

Efes Pilsener Premium 5% abv

The Premium gets its pale yellow-gold colour and texture from the bright Pils malt used in its production. It has a musty, grainy aroma and a peppery and spicy flavour with average length and a reasonably hoppy finish.

Efes Pilsener Light 2.7% abv

This is a pale straw colour with a subtle aroma and a refreshing texture. It is crisp with a soft, malty palate at the front, which fades to some dryness on the short finish.

Efes Pilsener Extra 7% abv

Brewed with 'extra' malt and hops, this beer has a rich and fruity aroma. It has a creamy texture and a full flavour carried through the entire palate to the finish by the generous alcohol level. Worthy of respect.

Efes Pilsener Dark 5% abv

A classic dark beer, deep brown in colour with a gently chocolate/caramel aroma. The flavour combines good malt character with a soft hop finish. The smooth texture and generous mouth-feel make this a very drinkable beer.

United Kingdom

1698 Celebration Ale 6.5% abv

Made with only Kentish hops, this beer is a golden honey colour with good mouth-feel and well-balanced fruit, hop and malt flavours. Plenty of length and a sweet dry finish.

Abbot Ale 5% abv

Rich, strong and robust with a distinct malt fruit and toffee flavour. Plenty of body and a lingering, slightly bitter-sweet finish.

Badger Country Bitter 4% abv

Mid-gold in colour with mild malt aroma. Good mouth-feel and full flavour of malt and green grass. Some herb and spice characters. Traditional bitter finish.

Bass Pale Ale 5% abv

A deep, rich, amber, traditionally brewed British pale ale with a full body and pleasant bitterness. A classic beer to match with steak and kidney pudding.

Belhaven St Andrew's Ale 4.6% abv

Rich and peppery hop aroma with fruit notes; full malt and nut flavour with good hop character. Balanced ale with intense, dry after-palate.

Bishops Finger Strong Ale 5.4% abv

Golden brown with a slight red hue, Bishop's Finger is full bodied with a creamy texture. Rich fruit and malt flavours dominate, providing a long finish and a sweet-toffee aftertaste.

Boddington's Pub Ale 4.8% abv

A classic British draught ale famous for its thick creamy head. Boddington's has a full-bodied, malty flavour that lingers through to a creamy, smooth finish.

Burton's Creamy Ale 4.2% abv

Very dark brown in colour, Burton's Creamy Ale is a visual delight — a mass of tiny bubbles disappear to produce a glass of crystal-clear, nut-brown beer capped by about 200 millimetres of creamy head. A chocolate/coffee flavour, full and rich, and a lengthy, semi-bitter finish.

Caffrey's Irish Ale 4.8% abv

Caffrey's was inspired by Thomas Caffrey, founder of the famous Mountain Brewery in Ireland. A creamy texture settles, tantalisingly slowly, to give a superb, smooth mouth-feel. A malty sweet flavour with a gentle, hoppy finish.

Double Diamond Burton Ale 5% abv

Brewed from pale chocolate malts. Good hop palate and refreshing pale ale style. Draughtflow can.

Fuller's London Pride 4.7% abv

A copper-coloured ale with an assertive, malty flavour, balancing hop bitterness and lingering fruit/hoppy flavour. Marvellous complexity with a high degree of fruitiness, hops and malt, with only medium bitterness. A hint of caramel is balanced nicely by the hops, which is noticeable only after it has warmed in your glass for a while. The finish is equally complex, with a smooth, lingering mellowness that's neither sweet nor dry — just memorable.

John Smith's Bitter 3.8% abv

Best drunk through its rich, creamy head, this beer is dark brown-amber in colour. It is creamy and full bodied with a distinctive, sharp, hop flavour and bitterness balanced by chocolate malts. Silky smooth to the finish.

King & Barnes Festive 5.3% abv

A bottle-conditioned beer, very hoppy with a herbal aroma and a big, smooth fruitiness.

McEwan's Export Pale Ale 4.5% abv

A provocative beer with a distinctive and unusual flavour. Smooth and crisp, it is moderately sweet with at the same time an interesting dryness that catches the back palate. Real character.

McEwan's Scotch Ale 8% abv

A very strong and rich winter warmer in the classic style. Deep brown-red in colour with a dark chocolate aroma and a full body. Smooth and full of malty flavours, with a slight, cleansing, hop finish.

McEwan's Lager 4.1% abv

Rich golden grain colour; hop aroma; crisp and clean texture; both malt and hop influence the flavour; balanced, satisfying finish.

McEwan's Export IPA 4.5% abv

Best served well chilled, this beer is the colour of dry hay. It has a mild aroma of grass and grain and a smooth, crisp texture and mouth-feel. There is definite malt in the flavour as well as a distinct roast-barley note. A refreshing, slightly bitter finish.

Master Brew 4% abv

A rich tan-brown, traditional ale with creamy texture, medium bitterness and a fuller flavour of mellow malt and caramel.

Newcastle Brown Ale 4.7% abv

An interesting and complex beer, clean and light, with a slightly roasted aroma and a smoky, nostalgic character and rich flavour. Good, simple brown ale style that will make a good session beer.

Old Speckled Hen 5.2% abv

Morland's Old Speckled Hen has a superb, rich, malty, estery aroma and a wonderful, mouth-filling, warming flavour bursting with body. Malt and toffee flavours combine with bitterness on the back of the tongue to give a balanced sweetness that is not cloying.

Original Porter Ale 5% abv

Deep chocolate-brown; malty fruit, Christmas-cake aroma; creamy mouth-filling body; full, rich chocolate and liquorice flavours. This is a meal of a beer, with character and a lengthy, satisfying, bitter-sweet finish.

Samuel Smith's Nut Brown Ale 5% abv

Malty and bitter; full of texture; nutty finish to the palate.

Samuel Smith's Old Pale Ale 5% abv

Generous aroma of hops with a smooth texture and a malty flavour. Good length.

Samuel Smith's Taddy Porter 5% abv

Similar to a dry stout but lighter in body. Quite fruity on the aroma and in flavour.

Samuel Smith's Imperial Stout 5% abv

Deep, deep chocolate-brown; rich, malt aroma with traces of toffee; good mouth-feel; rich, complex finish.

Spitfire Bitter Ale 5.5% abv

Mid-straw in colour with a dominating hop aroma, Spitfire Bitter Ale has a crisp, dry texture and lightweight mouth-feel. The hops come through again on the palate, with some cut-grass and some hay influence providing both hop bitterness and a lingering, dry aftertaste.

Tanglefoot 5% abv

Very pale straw colour with an equally light texture and moderate mouth-feel. Good balance of flavours showing generous hop. Dry rather than bitter.

Tennent's Lager 5% abv

Yellow-gold in colour, this beer has a mild straw-like aroma with some yeastiness. Full bodied but clean and crisp, the flavour has malty accents and is somewhat fruity with mild hop influence.

Tennent's Super Lager 9% abv

One of the strongest lagers brewed in the United Kingdom, Tennent's Super is light gold in colour and appreciably strong in taste, with lengthy hop flavour and bitterness balanced by some welcome malt character. A small glass of this weighty brew makes a fine digestive.

Tetley Export Bitter 5% abv

Full-strength bitter beer. Rich, creamy flavour; good malt and hops balance; dry finish; in-can nitrogenised Draughtflow system.

Theakston's Old Peculiar 6% abv

A strong Yorkshire ale with deep dark-brown colour and rich body. Moderately sweetish and well-rounded with a fresh, lighter-than-expected flavour that has smoky, meaty-bacon influences. Smooth and satisfying with a long, rich, concentrated palate.

Theakston's Best Bitter 3.8% abv

Another to drink through its head. A creamy, full-bodied texture with a clean edge to it. The flavour is full with malt and a touch of yeast character. Very mouth-filling, with a generous finish.

United States

Bad Frog Original 4.5% abv

A golden amber beer with a smooth but distinct, rich, malt character resulting from the long cold-maturation time. It has a moderate length.

Bad Frog Lemon Lager 3.25% abv

An extremely light and smooth beer with a refreshing hint of lemon. A favourite with lager and lime fans.

Blackened Voodoo Lager 4.95% abv

Deep amber-rose colour, and pleasant malt and hop aroma. Big, dry-toasted malt flavour with some hops in the back and a dry hop aftertaste. This is an all-malt beer made from five different malts and Mt Hood and Cascade hops.

Budweiser 5% abv
Another lightweight, light straw-coloured beer, with a sweet aroma and very little mouth-feel. Mild honey and tropical fruit flavour, uncomplicated by hop influences. No finish to speak of.

Dixie Lager 4.5% abv
Gold with a touch of amber, lightly hopped with a slightly sour malt aroma. Light body; refreshing hop flavour; medium-dry finish and aftertaste.

Lone Star 4.6% abv
Gold; light malt and hop aroma; flavour to match light body; medium-dry finish with little aftertaste.

Miller Genuine Draft 4.7% abv
Miller is the top-selling US beer in New Zealand. Straw-gold in colour, it has a malty aroma with floral tones and plenty of sweetness in the flavour. A light, refreshing quaffer.

Glossary

This glossary was compiled using definitions supplied by the American Beer Masters Tasting Society. The profiles applied to particular beer styles (bock, pilsener, stout, etc.) are very general. There are commonly many variations of each style which highlight differences between countries, brewing preferences and ingredients.

ADJUNCT fermentable material used as a substitute for traditional grains to make beer lighter-bodied or cheaper

ABV (ALCOHOL BY VOLUME) amount of alcohol in beer in terms of percentage volume of alcohol per volume of beer

ACIDIC (see sour)

ALCOHOLIC warming taste of ethanol and higher alcohols

ALE beer distinguished by use of top-fermenting yeast strains. Top-fermenting yeasts perform at warmer temperatures than yeasts used to brew lager beer, and their by-products are more evident in taste and aroma. Fruitiness and esters are often part of an ale's character.

AMBER a colour between pale and dark brown, with a hint of red

AROMA HOPS varieties of hop chosen to impart bouquet

ASTRINGENT a drying, puckering taste; tannic. It can be derived from boiling the grains, long mashes, over-sparging or sparging with hard water.

BARLEY a cereal grain that is malted for use in the grist that becomes the mash in the brewing of beer

BITTERNESS the perception of a bitter flavour, in beer derived from hops or malt husks; a sensation on the back of the tongue

BLACK MALT partially malted barley roasted at high temperatures; black malt gives a dark colour and roasted flavour to beer

BOCK beer distinguished by copper to dark brown colour; full body; malty sweet character dominating the aroma and flavour with a hint of chocolate; low bitterness; low hop flavour; no hop aroma; no fruitiness or esters; low to medium diacetyl is okay

BODY thickness and mouth-filling property of a beer

BOTTLE CONDITIONING secondary fermentation and maturation in the bottle, creating complex aromas and flavours

BREWHOUSE the equipment used to make beer

BREW-PUB a pub that makes beer and sells at least half of it on the premises. Known in the United Kingdom as a home-brew house and in Germany as a house brewery.

BUTTERSCOTCH see diacetyl

CARBONATION sparkle caused by carbon-dioxide, either created during fermentation or injected later

CARAMEL a cooked sugar that is used to add colour and alcohol content to beer, often used in place of more expensive malted barley

CARAMEL MALT a sweet, copper-coloured malt imparting both colour and flavour to beer. It has a high concentration of unfermentable sugars that sweetens the beer and contributes to head retention.

CASK a closed, barrel-shaped container for beer, available in various sizes and now usually made of metal. The bung in a cask of 'real' beer or ale must be made of wood to allow the pressure to be relieved, as the fermentation of the beer in the cask continues.

CASK CONDITIONING secondary fermentation and maturation in the cask at the point of sale. It creates light carbonation.

CHILL-HAZE cloudiness caused by precipitation of protein-tannin compound at low temperatures; does not affect flavour

CLOVE-LIKE spicy character reminiscent of cloves, present in some wheat beers; if excessive it may derive from wild yeast

CONDITIONING period of maturation intended to impart 'condition' (natural carbonation). Warm conditioning further develops the complex of flavours; cold conditioning imparts a clean, round taste.

CONTRACT BEER beer made by one brewery and then marketed by a company calling itself a brewery; the latter uses the brewing facilities of the former

DIACETYL a volatile compound in beer that contributes to a butterscotch flavour, measured in parts per million

DRY-HOPPING the addition of dry hops to fermenting or ageing beer to increase its hop character or aroma

ESTER a volatile flavour compound, often fruity, flowery or spicy, naturally created in fermentation

FERMENTATION conversion of sugars into ethyl alcohol and carbon-dioxide through the action of yeast

FRUITY flavour and aroma of bananas, strawberries, apples or other fruit; caused by high-temperature fermentation and certain yeast strains

GRAINY tasting like cereal or raw grain

HAND PUMP a device for dispensing draught beer operated by hand. The use of a hand pump allows cask-conditioned beer to be served without the use of pressurised carbon-dioxide.

HEFE a German word meaning 'with', used mostly in conjunction with wheat (weiss) beers to denote that the beer is bottled or kegged with the yeast in suspension (hefe-weiss). These beers are cloudy, frothy and very refreshing.

HOPS herb added to boiling wort or fermenting beer to impart a bitter aroma and flavour

INDIA PALE ALE pale to deep amber or copper colour; medium body; medium maltiness; high hop bitterness; medium to high hop flavour and aroma; fruity, estery character; alcohol strength evident; low diacetyl is okay

LAGER beer produced with bottom-fermenting yeast strains at colder fermentation temperatures than an ale. The cooler environment inhibits the natural production of esters and other by-products, creating a crisper-tasting product.

LAMBIC-STYLE ALE intensely and cleanly sour; no hop bitterness, flavour or aroma; fruity, estery character; uniquely aromatic; effervescent. Malted barley and unmalted wheat and stale, old hops are used. Cloudiness is acceptable.

LIGHT-STRUCK a skunk-like smell resulting from exposure to light

LIQUOR the water used in the brewing process, as included in the mash or used to sparge the grains after mashing

MAINSTREAM mass-produced beer enjoyed by many New Zealanders. Generally it is malt, sweetish, only lightly hopped with a moderately firm body, little aftertaste and no great palate-challenging characteristics. Line a few mainstream beers up and most drinkers would find it difficult to spot identify 'their' brand.

MALT the grain, usually barley, used as the foundation ingredient of beer

MALTING the process by which barley is steeped in water, germinated then kilned to convert insoluble starch to soluble substances and sugar

MEDICINAL chemical or phenolic character; can be the result of wild yeast, or contact with plastic or sanitiser residue

METALLIC tasting tinny, blood-like or coin-like; may come from bottle caps

MOUTH-FEEL a sensation derived from the consistency or viscosity of a beer

MUSTY mouldy, mildewy character; can be the result of cork or bacterial infection

OXIDISED stale flavour of wet cardboard, paper, rotten pineapple or sherry, as a result of oxygen affecting the beer as it ages or is exposed to high temperatures

PASTEURISATION heating of beer to 60–79°C to stabilise it microbiologically. Flash-pasteurisation is applied very briefly, for 15–60 seconds, by heating the beer as it passes through the pipe. Alternatively, bottled beer can be passed on a conveyor belt through a heated tunnel; this more gradual process takes at least 20 minutes and sometimes much longer.

PET North Island term for a 2-litre plastic container commonly used by customers to collect beer from a brewery. Known in the South Island as a rigger.

PILSENER (PILSNER) colour is pale to golden; light to medium body; high hop bitterness; medium hop flavour and aroma; low maltiness in aroma and flavour; no fruitiness or esters; very low diacetyl is okay

PORTER black colour; no roasted barley character; sharp bitterness of black malt without much burnt or charcoal-like flavour; medium to full body; malty sweetness; hop bitterness

medium to high; zero to medium hop flavour and aroma; fruity, estery character is okay, as is low diacetyl

RIGGER South Island term for a 2-litre plastic or glass container, in the North Island called a pet and sometimes a flagon

SALTY flavour like table salt, experienced on the side of the tongue

SECONDARY FERMENTATION stage of fermentation occurring in a closed container, lasting from several weeks to several months

SHELF LIFE the length of time a beer will retain its peak drinkability. The shelf life for commercially produced beers is usually a maximum of four months.

SOUR/ACIDIC vinegar-like or lemon-like; can be caused by bacterial infection

SPARGE to spray grist with hot water in order to remove soluble sugars (maltose); this takes place at the end of the mash

STOUT black, opaque colour; light to medium body; medium to high hop bitterness; roasted barley (coffee-like) character; sweet maltiness and caramel malt evident; no hop flavour or aroma; slight acidity/sourness is okay; low to medium alcohol; low to medium diacetyl

SWEET tasting like sugar; experienced on the front of the tongue

SULPHUR-LIKE reminiscent of rotten eggs or burnt matches; a by-product of some yeasts

TARTNESS taste sensation cause by acidic flavours

VINOUS reminiscent of wine

WINEY sherry-like flavour caused by warm fermentation or oxidation in very old beer

YEASTY yeast-like flavour; a result of yeast in suspension or beer sitting too long on sediment

References

Aidells, B. and Kelly, D., *Real Beer and Good Eats*, Knopf, New York, 1995
Gordon, D., *Speight's: The Story of Dunedin's Historic Brewery*, Avon, Dunedin, 1993
Jackson, M., *Beer*, Penguin, London, 1998
Jackson, M., *Beer Companion*, Running Press, Philadelphia, 1994
Jackson, M., *The New World Guide to Beer*, Running Press, Philadelphia, 1988
McLauchlan, G., *The Story of Beer*, Viking, Auckland, 1994
Saunders, L., *Cooking with Beer*, Time Life Books, Virginia, 1996

There are any number of excellent beer and brewing sites on the World Wide Web. Amongst the best are www.beermasters.com and www.realbeer.com. Another site of interest to New Zealanders is www.brewing.co.nz.

Sparging: The New Zealand Brewers News is available from PO Box 39-234, Howick, Auckland.

Index

1698 Celebration Ale 160

Abbot Ale 160
ABC Stout 157
Albert Brewery 37
Alexander, Steve 27
Allen, Martin 128
Anchor Pilsener Beer 157
Armstrong, Keith 101
Asahi Super Dry 155
Auckland Breweries 17, 51
Auckland Dark 52, *134*
Auckland Draught 52, *134*
Auckland Lager 52, *134*
Australis Brewing Company 17, 42

Bad Frog Lemon Lager 165
Bad Frog Original 165
Badger Country Bitter 160
Banner, Tracy 91
Baroona Berry 23, *130*
Baroona Dark Ale 24, *130*
Baroona Original 23, *130*
Baroona Spring Pale Ale 24
Barraclough Lager 33
Bass Pale Ale 160
Bavaria 'Edel' Lager 158
Bays Dark Ale 88, *138*
Bays Draught Ale 87, *138*
Bays Gold Lager 87, *138*
Beamish Irish Stout 154
Beamish Red Ale 154
Bean Rock Brewing Company 17, 29
Bean Rock Lager 30, *131*
Becks 152
Delhaven St Andrew's Ale 160
Belle Vue Framboise 148
Belle Vue Gueuze 148
Belle Vue Kriek 148
Bellringers Bitter 41, *132*

Benediction Belgian Abbey-Style Ale
42, *133*
Betteridge, Hamish 61
Bishops Finger Strong Ale 161
Bitburger Premium 152
Bitter and Twisted 41
Black Bier 109, *142*
Black Brute Stout 28, *131*
Black Gold 82
Black Mac 93, *139*
Black Magic 61, *135*
Black Rat Dark Ale 26, *130*
Black Robin Brewery 81, 82
Black Shag Stout 107, *142*
Blackened Voodoo Lager 165
Blue Duck Draught 106, *141*
Bob Hudson's Bitter 40, *132*
Boddington's Pub Ale 161
Bretherton, Simon 112
Brew Haus 17, 61
Brew Haus Dark Ale 62
Brew Haus Lager 62
Brew Haus Pilsener 62
Brew Haus Weiss Beer 63, *135*
Brew Hause Malt Ale 62
Brewer's Daughter, The 85
Brewhouse Dark, The 71
Brewhouse Draught, The 71
Brewhouse Lager, The 70
Brewhouse, The 17, 70
Brewski 118, *143*
Brofords Beers 17, 27
Brofords Western Bitter 28, *131*
Brofords Western Lager 28, *131*
Buchanan's Special Dark Ale 28, *131*
Budejovicky Budvar 151
Budweiser 166
Burke, John 19
Burke, Rodney 111

Burkes Bitter 20, *130*
Burkes Kaipara Brewery 17, 19
Burridges Brewery 17, 74
Burridges Brown Jug 75, *136*
Burridges Lansdowne Lager 75, *136*
Burton's Creamy Ale 161

Cadman, Gordon 57
Caffrey's Irish Ale 161
Canterbury Brewery (New Zealand
  Breweries) 81, 110
Canterbury Draught 110, *142*
Canterbury Independent Brewery
  81, 108
Captain Cooker Manuka Beer 84, *138*
Carlsberg Green 151
Carlton Cold Filtered Beer 145
Carlton Stripe 145
Carrad, Innes 18
Cascade Premium Lager 146
Castle Lager 158
Castle Rock Black 116
Castle Rock Brewing 81, 114
Castle Rock Draught 115
Castle Rock Extra 115
Castle Rock Gold Lager 115
Castle Rock Wheat 115
Charles Stolberg Premium Reserve Lager
  29, *131*
Chimay Blue Trappist Ale 149
Chimay Red Trappist Ale 149
Chimay White Trappist Ale 149
Classic Black 119, *143*
Classic Draft 54
Coachman's Ale 18, *129*
Coastal Breweries 17, 65
Coastal Draught 66
Cock & Bull English Pub 53
Cock & Bull Lager 54
Collier, Glen 76
Cooper's Best Extra Stout 146
Cooper's Original Pale Ale 146
Cooper's Premium Clear Ale 146
Cooper's Sparkling Ale 146
Cope, Brian 117
Cork & Keg 95

Corona Extra 156
Crater Ale 26, *130*

Dark Horse Stout 84, *137*
Dark Star 56
Davies, Tony 66
Day, Carl 30
DB Bitter 49, *133*
DB Breweries *see* Mainland Brewery;
  Monteith's Brewery; Tui Brewery;
  Waitemata Brewery
DB Draught 117, *143*
DB Export Dry 49, *133*
DB Natural 49, *133*
DB Natural Light 50, *134*
Denny, Tony 56
Diamond 147
Dixie Lager 166
Dixon, Andrew 82
Double Diamond Burton Ale 161
Dowling, Jim 20
Duff, Gavin 120
Duff's Brewery 81, 120
Duffs Classic Gold Wheat Lager 120, *143*
Duffs Dark Ale 121, *143*
Duffs Edinburgh Draught Ale 121, *143*
Duffs Special Draught 120
Duke, John 44
Duncan, John 85
Duncan, Nick 116
Duncan's Founders Brewery 81, 85
Duvel Top Fermented Strong Beer 149
Dux de Lux 81, 105
Dux Lager 106, *141*

Efes Pilsener Dark 160
Efes Pilsener Extra 159
Efes Pilsener Light 159
Efes Pilsener Premium 159
Egmont Pale Ale 65, *136*
Elephant Beer 151
Emerson Brewing Company, The
  81, 124
Emerson, Richard 124
Emerson's 1812 India Pale Ale 125, *144*
Emerson's Bookbinder Bitter 126
Emerson's London Porter 127, *144*

Emerson's 'Old 95' 127, *144*
Emerson's Pilsener 125, *144*
Emerson's Weissbier Dunkel 126, *144*
Emerson's Weissbier Hefe-Weizenbier
    125, *144*
Emerson's Whisky Porter 126
Export Gold 49, *133*

Falstaff's Real Ale 34
Fife, Richard 105
Finnegans Traditional Dark Ale 105, *141*
Flame Beer 51
Flying Horse Royal Lager 153
Forge Draught 108, *142*
Foster's Lager 147
Foster's Light 147
Foster's Special Bitter 147
Tuggles Best Bitter 54, *134*
Fuller's London Pride 161

Galbraith Brewing Company 17, 40
Galbraith, Keith 40, 42
Galbraith's Ale House 23, 40, 42
Gerard, Nigel 128
Gillies, Dave 117
Giraf Gold 151
Gisborne Bitter 60, *135*
Gisborne Gold 60, *135*
Golden Goose Lager 83, *137*
Graff, Manfred 128
Grafton Porter 41, *132*
Great Northern Brewery 37
Greig, Colin 73
Grolsch 157
Guinness 111

Hagerty, Steve 119
Harleys Premium Ale 88, *138*
Harrington, Craig 88
Harrington's Best Bitter 89, *138*
Harrington's Big John 112, *142*
Harrington's Brewery (Christchurch)
    81, 112; (Nelson) 81, 88
Harrington's Canterbury Pale Ale 113, *142*
Harrington's Draught 114, *143*
Harrington's Finest Lager (Christchurch)
    113, *143*; (Nelson) 89, *138*
Harrington's Kiwi Draught 113, *143*

Harrington's Lager 113, *142*
Harrington's Stout 90, *139*
Harrington's Tasman Lager 90, *139*
Harrington's Traditional Dark 114, *143*
Harrington's Wheat Beer 90, *139*
Harrison, Adrian 74
Harrison, Chris 68
Hauslager Gold Label 108, *142*
Heineken 50, *134*
Hereford Bitter 106, *141*
Hite Beer 156
Hodgson India Pale Ale 43, *133*
Hoegaarden Forbidden Fruit 149
Hoegaarden Grand Cru 149
Hoegaarden White 149
Hog Dark Ale 31, *131*
Hog Draft Beer 31, *131*
Hog Gold Lager 31, *131*
Hog Wheat Beer 32, *131*
Hogan, Paul 108
Hokianga Breweries 17, 18
Holling, Mike 116
Holsten Premium 152
Hooker Ale 29
Hop Head Pale Ale 55
Hosking, Daniel 71
Howard, Peter 104
Hoyle, Dave 27
Hurricane Premium 96

Ice 37, 132
Independent Brewery (Auckland) 17, 56;
    (Napier) 17, 66
Island Draught 82
Island Gold 82

John Smith's Bitter 162
Johnson, Mike 63

Kahikatea Best Bitter 59, *135*
Kahikatea Brewery 17, 57
Kahikatea Cold Gold 58, *134*
Kahikatea Dark Ale 58, *135*
Kahikatea Draught 58, *135*
Kaiapoi Brewery 81, 104
Kaiapoi Draught 105, *141*
Kaipara Gold Lager 19, *129*
Kaipara Olde Ale 20, *129*

Kaltenberg 'Royal' Lager 159
Kalyani Export Special 154
Kilkenny 111
King & Barnes Festive 162
King Lear Old Ale 35, *132*
Kingfisher Premium Lager 154
Kirin 155
Knight, Alan 22
Kostritzer Schwarzbier 152
Kronenbourg 152
Kumar, Charles 35

Labatts Blue 150
Lamplough, Dean 99
Lava Lager 25, *130*
Lava Lite 27, *131*
Leffe Blonde 150
Leopard Black Label 39, *132*
Light Ice 37, *132*
Lighthouse Brewery 81, 85
Lighthouse Classic Stout 86, *138*
Lighthouse Dark Ale 86, *138*
Lighthouse Lager 86, *138*
Lion Breweries (New Zealand Breweries)
     17, 37
Lion Brown 39, *132*
Lion Red 38, *132*
Littlejohn, Stuart 121
Loaded Hog Brewery, The (Auckland) 17,
     30; (Christchurch) 81, 111; (Wellington)
     17, 80
Logan, Geoff 59
Lone Star 166
Lowenbrau Original 152

Macbeth's Real Ale 34
McCashin's Brewery & Malthouse 91
McCrorie, Nathan 82, 95
McEwan's Export IPA 162
McEwan's Export Pale Ale 162
McEwan's Lager 162
McEwan's Scotch Ale 162
McLean, Mike 30
McNeills Cottage Brewery 81, 119
Mac's Ale 92, *139*
Mac's Extra 93, *139*
Mac's Gold 91, *139*

Mac's Premium Reserve 92, *139*
Mac's Special Light 92, *139*
Mainland Brewery (DB Breweries) 81, 116
Malthouse Brewery & Bar, The 17, 35
Malthouse Dark 36
Malthouse Lager 36
Malthouse Real Ale 36
Mammoth 98, *140*
Marlborough Brewing Company 81, 93
Marlborough Draught 94, *139*
Marlborough Gold 94, *139*
Mason, Rick 18
Master Brew 163
Mates Amber 67
Mates Dark 67
Mates Draught 67, *136*
Mates Gold 67, *136*
Matson's Classic Draught 109, *142*
Matson's Strong Ale 109, *142*
Maude, Gerry 59
Meenan Extra Strong Ale 122, *144*
Meenan Finest Best Bitter 122, *144*
Meenan High Country Draught 122, *144*
Meenan Lager 122, *143*
Meenan Wines & Spirits 81, 121
Middlemass, Ben 42
Mike's Mild Ale 64, *135*
Milkshed Brewing Company 128
Miller Genuine Draft 166
Miner's Brewery 81, 99
Miner's Classic Gold 100, *140*
Miner's Dark 101, *140*
Miner's Draught 100, *140*
Monks Habit 55, *134*
Monteith's Black 103, *141*
Monteith's Bock Winter Bier 103, *141*
Monteith's Brewing Company
     (DB Breweries) 81, 101
Monteith's Celtic Red 102, *141*
Monteith's Golden Lager 102, *141*
Monteith's Original Ale 102, *141*
Monteith's Pilsner 103, *141*
Monteith's Summer Ale 104, *141*
Moonlight Ale 119, *143*
Moonshine Strong Pilsener 60, *135*
Moosehead 150

Murphy's Irish Stout 155
Murray, Phil 48
Mussel Inn 81, 82

Nelson Bays Brewery 81, 87
New Zealand Breweries *see* Canterbury
   Brewery; Lion Breweries; Speight's
   Brewery
New Zealand Lager 56, *134*
Newcastle Brown Ale 163
Newcombe, Brett 87
Newman, Barry 32
Nicholas, Luke 53
Northland Breweries 17, 18
Northland Draught *129*
Northland Lager *129*
Northland Old Ale *129*
Nor'wester Strong Pale Ale (Christchurch)
   107, *142*; (Lower Hutt) 77, *137*

Oades, Amanda 25
O'Leary, Chris 68
O'Neill, Brian & Helen 64
O'Neills Black Peat 64, *135*
O'Neills Brewing Company 17, 64
O'Neills Special Lager 65, *135*
Old Black Strong Winter Stout 47, *133*
Old Speckled Hen 163
Old Thumper Robust Malt Beer 46, *133*
Onehunga Spring Brewery 17, 46
Oranjeboom Premium Lager 157
Original Manuka Honey Beer 22
Original Porter Ale 163
Original Steam Beer 95, *140*

Pachyderm Stout 98, *140*
Parrot & Jigger 17, 76
PBA 99, *140*
PDA 98, *140*
Peroni Nastro Azzuro 155
Petone Brewery 128
Pilot Bay Amber 21, *130*
Pilot Bay Brewing Company 17, 20
Pilot Bay Dark 21, *130*
Pilot Bay Lager 21, *130*
Pilsner Urquell 151
Pink Elephant Brewery 81, 97
Pink, Roger 97

Piston Draught 77, *137*
Polar Brewery 17, 78
Polar Dark 79, *137*
Polar Draught 79, *137*
Polar India Pale Ale 78, *137*
Polar Lager 79, *137*
Polar White Beer 80
Power's Bitter 147

Raffles Lager 158
Ramsay, Ian 46
Ranfurly Draught 57, *134*
Rangitoto Brewing Company 17, 25
Raspberry Rat 26, *131*
Raunchenfelser Steinbier 153
Red Devil 94, *139*
Red Stripe Lager 155
Redjacks Brewing Company 81, 116
Renwick Breweries 81, 95
Renwick Natural Draught 96, *140*
Renwick Original Dark 96, *140*
Renwick Pilsner Lager 96, *140*
Resch's Pilsener 147
Rheineck Lager 38, *132*
Roc Mac 81, 91
Romanov Baltic Stout 43, *133*
Romerkrug 'Stein' 153
Ronson, Brian 57
Roosters Brewhouse 17, 68
Roosters Dark Ale 70, *136*
Roosters Draught 69, *136*
Roosters Golden Wheat 69, *136*
Roosters Haymaker 68, *136*
Roosters Lager 69, *136*
Roosters Pale Blonde 69

Samuel Smith's Imperial Stout 164
Samuel Smith's Nut Brown Ale 163
Samuel Smith's Old Pale Ale 163
Samuel Smith's Taddy Porter 164
Sapporo Premium Lager 155
Schneider Aventinus Weiss Doppelbock 153
Schneider Weiss Bier (helle) Original 153
Scottish Wee Heavy 22, *130*
Sel's Ice Beer 45
Sel's Pub Dark 45
Sel's Pub Draft 44

Sel's Pub Lager 44
Sel's Super 45
Shakespeare Draught 33
Shakespeare Tavern & Brewery 17, 32
Shamrock Brewing Company 17, 71
Shamrock Dark 72
Shamrock Draught 72
Shamrock Lager 73
Shamrock Stout 73
Shamrock Strong Bitter 72
Shaw, Nigel 51
Shylock's Light 33
Silver Fern New Zealand Lager 46, *133*
Singha 159
Sol 156
Southman's Draught 97, *140*
Sou'wester Strong Dark Stout
   (Christchurch) 107, *142*; (Lower Hutt)
   77, *137*
Speight's Brewery (New Zealand
   Breweries) 9, 123
Speight's Distinction Ale 124, *144*
Speight's Gold Medal Ale 123, *144*
Speight's Old Dark Malt Ale 124, *144*
Spitfire Bitter Ale 164
Spring Brewery Natural Draught 47, *133*
Spring Brewery Natural Lager 47, *133*
Spring Natural Red Ale 47
Steam Brewing Company 17, 53
Steinlager 39, *132*
Stella Artois 150
Stephens, Rob 93
Stoddart, Alistair 128
Stoker Dark 77, *137*
Street Pauli Girl 153
Strong Ox 84, *138*
Sundowner Dark Ale 60, *135*
Sunshine Brewing Company 17, 59
Super Dry 50, *134*
Swan Special Light 147

Tafel Lager 156
Tall Black 118, *143*

Tanglefoot 164
Tarawera Draught 53, *134*
Taylor, Peter 65
Tennent's Lager 164
Tennent's Super Lager 164
Tetley Export Bitter 165
Theakston's Best Bitter 165
Theakston's Old Peculiar 165
Thompson, Leigh 82
Tiger 158
Tooheys Blue Label 148
Tout, Dick 85
Trident Tavern 17, 44
Tsing Tao 150
Tuborg Gold 152
Tui Brewery (DB Breweries) 17, 73
Tui East India Pale Ale 74, *136*
Twin Pines Brew House 128

Valley Pale 76
Vasta, Carl 78
Victoria Bitter 148

Waiheke Island Microbrewery 17, 22
Waiheke Winter Warmer 24
Waikato Draught 38, *132*
Wairarapa Brewer's Draught 75, *137*
Waitemata Brewery (DB Breweries)
   17, 48
Wakatipu Gold Lager 119, *143*
Wanaka Beerworks 81, 117
Warsteiner Premium 153
Watson, Brian 29
Wests Cordials 128
Whinham, Brendan 70
White Cliffs Brewing Company 17, 63
White Heron Wheat Beer 84, *138*
Wieblitz, Glen 114
Willpower Stout 34
Windhoek Lager 156
Windhoek Light 157

Zhujiang Beer 150